YOUR
FEARLESS
Soul

7 DIVINE PURPOSE TYPES.
What Will Yours Be?

CHRISTIN MYRICK

Birdhouse Publishing, LLC
Boulder, CO 80305

Printed in the United States of America

First Printing: November 2015

Cover Illustration Pixabay.com
Author Photo by Taylor Kokora

ISBN-978-0-9969807-0-8

Books may be purchased in quantity and/or special sales by contacting
info@birdhousepublishing.com

www.ChristinMyrick.com

For you, dear reader.
Here's to the unveiling of your Fearless Soul,
may it grow ever more wild and free.

Thank you for your Fearless Soul!
The world needs it.

With great heart,

CYprick

TABLE OF CONTENTS

PREFACE

My Fearless Soul Story

very person's story has the same essential thread: we each come into the world with authentic wildness, we go through a banishment that creates a survival mask, then we face our fears and return to the Fearless Soul.

The Fearless Soul System and the seven types of divine purpose I describe in this book are born from my own story, which I would like to share with you here to provide background and context for the work. I wrote this book to help me heal, forgive, and remember my own Fearless Soul. My hope is that it will help you do the same and, in turn, uncover the divine purpose that only you can give to the world.

My Authentic Wildness

I was born to parents who loved me. I was lucky in this regard. I know all parents love their children, but I was my parents' entire world. They were a young military couple who laughed easily and fell in love even easier. When my father proposed on the state line, he gave my mother a gold band with his nickname for her engraved on the inside: "Sweets."

They divorced when I was too young to remember, but they both contributed to my authentic wildness in very different ways. My mother was a beautiful creature, wild at heart, and life with her was rich and intense. It was just the two of us for a long time, living in our tiny cabin in the Alaskan woods where everything was an adventure. She taught me to be strong and resourceful—to leverage what I had in order to do what I needed to do. My father was a dreamer and a hopeless romantic. From my father I inherited a squishy-nougat-center and the humility to open my Soul to mystery.

I was a lighthearted, physical little person. I enjoyed moving my body and being inside cabinets. I liked to touch and smell and taste everything, and was curious to the point of being obnoxious. *(What's ozone? Where does the river go? Yeah, but where does it GO? Why aren't dinosaurs in the Bible?* It went on and on.)

I could always feel deeply into my environment, viscerally feel experiences and emotions of others in my body as if they were my own. I could comprehend what others really meant or wanted regardless of the words they used. It was like being tuned into a radio station that no one else could hear; I couldn't understand why adults would intentionally negate feelings that were so loudly broadcast. Like when said they were "fine" while there really was something troubling brewing inside, or when I talked to one parent about the other and they would tremor out an emotion that I could feel but was too young to understand (Remorse? Longing? Guilt?). It was a difficult experience to work with because I assumed all people viscerally experienced others to the degree that I did. All these quirks and intricacies were simply who I was born to be. I didn't know any other way to exist.

My Banishment

Banishment began for me when my mother asked for my blessing for her to marry again. My six-year-old intuition had recesses of doubt: something *felt* wrong. At the same time I could *feel* my mother's desire and fear of my rejection all tangled up together like lovers' limbs. They surged inside of her and therefore inside of me, and I couldn't bear to see her so troubled. I consented and they married shortly after.

I came to think of my step-father as an unrelenting storm: some days were better than others, but it was always raining. Sometimes he was a loving drunk, but more frequently he was violent and cruel—hurling words that stung far longer than any physical attack ever did. I learned to bury my opinions, thoughts, and feelings because displaying emotion invited shame. I learned to wear an obedient exterior because any strength of will received punishment. I learned silence because curiosity was attacked. There was also a disturbing flavor of sexual abuse from a family friend that cloaked my natural sensuality with a shroud of physical deadness (I couldn't, for example, feel sensation below my torso).

My ability to perceive what someone wanted or was really trying to say served me well in navigating this muddy terrain. I could guess, for example, with a high level of accuracy what kind of night laid ahead for me by the way the car door slammed in the garage. I could *feel* when he wanted me to cry or to fight back. Although much of my ability to sense my environment was natural, concentrated fear magnified it greatly. The connection, the depth of *feeling*, became so overwhelming in this environment that any curiosity in or joy for the world around me dissipated. I lost the connection with my own inner, emotional life and became numb in every way a person can be.

With each turn of our abusive cycle, my step-father's unstable behavior increased. First it was slapping and shoving, then dragging down stairs, punching out windows, throwing, midnight tirades, chasing me with bloody fists as I ran with my baby brother in my arms, and fingers constricting my neck. After one particular incident, his eyes went beyond rage and into a dark place that I couldn't recognize. His ability to reason emancipated and I wasn't sure that he would stop. It was then I knew that I had to leave.

But by then my sensitive heart had shattered and I couldn't pick up the pieces before I left. My body fled, but those pieces of me remained back in that house and in that time. In departing, and for a long time after, I felt nothing. There was nothing left to feel and there was nothing left of me to feel it. Numbness was my survival mechanism, helping me get through my banishment period. Unfortunately, it also eclipsed the wildness of my Soul. I became lost behind that unfeeling mask and the person I had once been had almost completely disappeared.

My Return and the Fearless Soul System

For many years, I wore only my survival mask until I met a man who made my Soul sing from the moment we met. Tall, lean, and quirky, he would disappear on his mountain bike for hours on end, retuning caked in mud and good humor. It had been a long time since I laughed so recklessly and cherished with such abandon. When he told me that he loved who I truly was (authentic wildness) but could not sustain a relationship with who I pretended to be (survival mask), I was shocked and hurt. Mostly I was afraid of the choice: I could either lose the love of my life or face my fears and return to my truest self. I chose the latter.

When we repress emotion or are unable to respond, a part of us gets stuck in that time and place. Going through my old fears and re-*feeling* was part of the process of collecting the pieces of my authentic wildness and bringing them home to present time. It was very triggering— meaning that there were many days that I could barely function: stuck in a panic attack, lost in a memory, unable to move or get out of bed.

My love stayed with me during this tumultuous revival. We considered every forward movement a major triumph: when I could be alone without feeling abandoned, when I could be angry without being mean, when he could touch my skin in the middle of the night and I wouldn't scream. We celebrated each as if I'd cured cancer—hugging and cheering, or going out for dinner. I won't say that my love saved me, because no one can save us from ourselves, but he did help me remember that I possessed the power to pull myself out of darkness and that I was worth saving.

In returning to authentic wildness, my world transitioned from black and white to Technicolor in every way. Sensation came into sharp relief and emotions were bittersweet. After so long of feeling nothing, now I was *feeling* everything and my ability to *feel* others (like I did as a child) increased exponentially. I was having difficulty controlling the depth of connection: I intimately connected with everyone instantaneously. It was delightful at first, but became increasingly overwhelming (no wonder my childhood self shut it off!).

This *feeling* ability is called being an empath,[1] which isn't a mystical talent, but something human beings possess in varying degrees of awareness and skill. I just happened to have a hyper-sensitive and, at the time, hyper-active empathy muscle.

Fortunately, a few dozen friends and acquaintances allowed me to slow my empathic process down and connect deeply with them in a more deliberate way. This taught me how to wade into the waters instead of high diving into the deep end. I called these sessions "Soul Seeings" because I *felt* into someone so deeply that I could "see" a metaphorical representation of their purpose, which was completely and intimately tied to the essence of who they really are. At the bottom of every connection was both a unique, authentic wildness and common motivations for what was bringing people to life. For example: some were oriented around authenticity and helping others be more real, others felt a powerful urge to protect and serve, and others created patterns out of chaotic information (much like myself). The more I felt and sensed people, the more a pattern emerged.

At first, each divine purpose was named after feelings or metaphors like "rising moon" or "blesser." The concepts weren't solid and they needed more tangible wording, so I used my empathy to feel into others and then asked them to describe and clarify their experience. I spent the next couple of years refining the names and abilities of the Fearless Soul System through

---

[1] "An empath is someone who is aware that he or she reads emotions, nuances, subtexts, undercurrents, intentions, thoughts, social space, interactions, relational behaviors, body language and gestural language to a greater degree than is deemed normal" (McLaren 5).

workshops and conversations, the bulk of which provided the depth and detail of content for this book.

The Fearless Soul System and the seven types of divine purpose came from my empathic experiences, facing fears, and retrieving lost pieces of my authentic wildness. What I discovered is that our Fearless Soul is always there, waiting to be uncovered. We simply have to dare enough to claim it.

INTRODUCTION

On a sunny summer day as a child I helped my auntie plant marigolds in her garden. We scooped the warm softness of earth into rows to hold the fragile seeds—each a tiny promise of beauty that would blossom and become. My final task was to attach the seed package label to a thin stick and insert it into the ground in front of the corresponding row. This is how my auntie would know which plants were in which row and then give them proper water and care. When we finished she looked back to find that I had placed all of the labels backwards, so that they were facing the garden and not the gardener. When my auntie asked me why, I replied, "So the seeds know what they're supposed to be."

It was a lovely thought for a small girl in a garden, helping the flowers grow with directions, but it does have one major flaw when applied to the realm of human behavior: it removes choice. There are giant labels all around us that tell us who we should be (labels like *full-time employee, stay at home mom, straight-A student,* or *rebel* to name a few). But you are the only person who can tell you who you truly are and what your deeper place of belonging in the world is.

It can be difficult to know who we truly are because, for most of us anyways, we were planted in the wrong row. Let's say you're a sunflower that has been planted in a row of beans. The label tells you that you are a bean plant and should produce beans. Everyone around you is a bean plant and they tell you to stick with the legume program. Even the gardener is absolutely certain that you are a bean plant because he planted you himself and tells you to quit misbehaving and start acting like a bean plant. But, no matter what you do, you will never be a bean plant.

You know you are different, somehow. Something in you is longing for the height of sun and sky, to reach your yellow petals into that infinite mystery of light. There is a whisper in your Soul that you cannot explain, but it calls to you like dreams fading in morning. You comprehend that this particular row, perhaps even this particular garden, is not your ultimate place of belonging. You know that your divine purpose is different than the other bean plants around you *because you feel it.*

The purpose of this book is to answer that whispering call of your Soul. To flip the labels of divine purpose around to face the garden and *to allow you to choose for yourself where you belong.* This book is for people who dare to ask, "Who am I?" It is written for those ready to face their fears, remove what does not bring them fully alive, and ultimately discover the divine purpose of their Souls.

What is Divine Purpose?

Everything has a place and a purpose: bean plants provide beans, sunflowers create seeds, rivers move water, trees make oxygen, and mushrooms decompose. Everything has a place and a purpose including you. Your divine purpose is meaningful contribution that only you can make. It is the way you belong to the world: your unique way of *being* for a *long* period of time.

Your divine purpose is deeper than a skill set or talent, deeper than personality or persona. Your divine purpose is not something you have to do. Throwing a baseball, writing cursive, connecting people, or writing computer code are things that you *do*. Your divine purpose aligns with the most essential part of who you are on the level of Soul. Divine purpose flows through you. A wild river bends and twists, churns rapids, and slowly meanders, but it is always the same river. You have strengths, weaknesses, skills, and talents but always the same divine purpose. To choose and claim your divine purpose is to have a truly Fearless Soul.

What is a Fearless Soul?

There is a story we each tell with our lives: we are born, we are banished, and we return. The characters, settings, themes, trials, and triumphs are different for each of us, but the underlying structure is the same.

Birth: We are born with essential qualities and talents that comprise our natural way of being. This is our *authentic wildness.*

Banishment: We are separated from our authentic wildness, and in this exile we learn to survive in the world via learned personality traits. This is our *survival mask.*

Return: We rediscover our authentic wildness, embrace our survival mask, and implement the benefits of each. The survival mask is no longer our primary response *but acts to consciously inform our authentic wildness*, and the two become one cohesive unit. This process requires that we face our fears and forgive. This is the *Fearless Soul*.

How to Use This Book

This book will not provide a test or an answer. It will not spoon-feed you a pre-packaged version of who you are and where you belong. The aim of this book is to help you orient toward one of the seven types of divine purpose in the Fearless Soul System that most resonates with the authentic, wild, natural version of you.

The seven types of divine purpose are named: Initiator, Messenger, Believer, Conduit, Guardian, Seer, and Converger. Part I of this book is dedicated to helping you identify your divine purpose type. This first section contains as many specific characteristics as possible because there is no test. There are no worksheets or external sources to tell you who you are. You get to decide which divine purpose most resonates with the essential nature of you. You may pick all of them, a few of them, one at a time—it doesn't matter. *What matters is that you feel out the divine purpose that best suits who you believe you are and commit to trying it on for a period of time.*

It is always possible to learn about, grow with, and utilize the divine purpose that may be different from your own. Your divine purpose type will simply be the one that is most natural to you and that you feel most at home in, but there is always room to explore and develop the others.

Part II will explain each divine purpose type in much greater detail. It will define the positive impact of each type and as well as suggestions of where to focus your energies so that you may start practicing immediately. It is important to note that each chapter in this section is laid out differently and utilizes different tones of voice meant to resonate with that divine purpose type. If you read multiple chapters to discover your divine purpose, you will notice this change. However, each chapter utilizes the same subheadings and you can use these as guideposts if you need to compare one type to another.

In Part III, we will discuss methods to apply your divine purpose and cultivate your Fearless Soul in tangible, immediate, and satisfying ways. As a final note, all names and some circumstances in the text have been altered in order to provide anonymity. It was my intention to convey the Fearless Soul of that person without compromising their privacy.

Like a whisper in the night, our Fearless Soul calls for us to return to who we really are so that its exquisite and enlivening nature can be revealed. No one else can be you, and no one else can provide your divine purpose to the world. Go deeper, dear reader. Remain attentive to what stirs inside and discover the call your Soul is longing to hear.

PART I

Your Fearless Soul

Ong namo.

Guru dev namo.

An opening mantra for some meditation practices,

which has many translations.

My favorite is:

I honor the subtle divine wisdom.

I surrender to the divine teacher within.

Chapter 1

YOUR AUTHENTIC WILDNESS

Authentic wildness is the root of your Fearless Soul.

A river begins as a slow, icy trickle high in the mountains. One droplet at a time cascades over faces of rock until they collect into a wide silver ribbon, which snakes its way through alpine valleys. These wild rivers revel in their space, with room to stretch watery limbs and flow effortlessly in tune with their authentic nature. Rivers were meant to be wild.

In urban settings, we don't see wild rivers. Our cities bind the streams in concrete channels or perfect arcs that move rigidly between blocks of manicured grass. Our infrastructure controls the natural waters and pipes them into straight, steel lines and right angles. And the river looses something precious—its wildness.

What we do to the rivers, we do to people too.

People begin as a slow, deliberate trickle of awakening. One moment at a time, we uncover the joy inherent in our bones. We are born loving rhythm, worshiping rain, and laughing without inhibition. As wild children, we revel in our own spaciousness, with room to stretch our curiosity and flow effortlessly in tune with our authentic natures. People are meant to be wild.

The older we get, the less frequently we see wild people. Our societal system binds the joy of our childhoods into cubed workspaces and perfect performance that moves rigidly between blocks of scheduled activity. Our system controls the natural flow of our authentic expression and pipes it into the straight and narrow definition of who we are "supposed" to be. And we lose something precious about ourselves in the process. We lose our wildness.

We exchange our authentic wildness for a sense of belonging to the world, but all we end up belonging to is a broken system.

If you are reading this book, the system does not work for you. You crave your authentic wildness with something akin to mania and you long

3

for the realness of a Fearless Soul. Having a Fearless Soul is not the absence of fear. The body and mind generate fear to let us know about danger. A Fearless Soul, rather, is *the willingness to be and express your authentic wildness to the best of your ability regardless of circumstance.* A Fearless Soul is completely alive in every moment and is the regenerative fullness of being who you truly are.

Who You Truly Are

You have unique traits and temperaments that do not change as you grow regardless of the environment you are raised in (Thomas). These inherent traits or qualities are the essential nature of who you are: your authentic wildness.

Your authentic wildness is as unique and innovative as you are. You may be grounded, empathic, and adventurous, or creative, lighthearted, and curious. None of these qualities are better or worse than the others, but it is important to understand your unique descriptors. They form the foundation of your Fearless Soul.

When I learned to play basketball as a teenager, I had to overcome my evident lack of talent and dexterity with tenacious practice. I would shoot the ball over and over again, but no matter what I did, I couldn't make a basket. Exasperated, my coach finally provided instruction on the concept of aim. "If you want to make a basket," she told me, "you have to aim for a corner of the square painted on the backboard, *not* the metal rim." I was skeptical, but gave it a go. I aimed for the corner and letting the ball fly. Sure enough, it bounced right off that corner and into the hoop with a delicious and satisfying swish.

Your authentic wildness and divine purpose work in much the same way. Typically, we tend to aim for things, experiences, jobs, or relationship to help us find meaning. This is the equivalent of aiming for the rim. Setting sights on a specific goal is not always the best method to achieve that goal. This is why your authentic wildness is so important. When you aim for the corner on the backboard, you make the shot. When you aim for fully expressing your authentic wildness, your divine purpose flows naturally and effortlessly. When you strive to be your truest self, a sense of purpose and happiness follow not because you are trying to do or achieve anything, but because it is *being who you truly are* that creates meaningful impact in the world.

Unearthing your authentic wildness is a life-long love affair, but the following exercise will get you started in the right direction.

Authentic Wildness Exercise

The goal of this exercise is to create a list of three to five qualities that describe your authentic wildness. To begin you will need a master list of qualities and traits. There are three ways you can create this master list:

1. Recall a moment in the near or distant past when you felt completely alive, connected, passionate, or loved. Many people have a strong experience of authenticity in childhood, but the moment could be much more recent than that. The important bit is to recollect a moment that *you felt most like yourself.* Begin to capture this moment on paper by writing a list of emotions, sensations, intuitions, or states of being that you experienced. (E.g. "I felt free, youthful, happy, wild, strong, warm, humorous, appreciative. . . .") Give yourself enough time to capture a complete list, only finishing when your answers do not come as easily as they did at first.

2. Ask someone who knew you before the age of four what you were like as a small child. Write down a list of the qualities that the other person uses to describe you, or have them create a list.

3. Ask a close friend or partner to share a favorite memory of you. We often find others attractive and full of life when they are acting in authentic wildness, so this is a fun way to capture your unique spark. You will fill up some of your love tanks *and* create a master list. Again, write down a list of qualities that the other person uses to describe you, or have them write the list.

4. A fourth option is to create a master list utilizing a combination of all three methods above.

    When your master list is complete, it is time to simplify it.

    Go through each entry and cross off anything that is impermanent. This includes your physical appearance, job, duties, relationships, age, position in the family, and even some emotional states. (E.g. "I felt sad" or "I was wearing blue shoes" would be temporary and therefore not relevant.)

5

Next cross off everything that you cannot take with you when you die. Remember, the purpose of this exercise is to help you claim the lasting blueprints of your unique Soul. You may find the exercise quick and effortless, or you may find it challenging and thought-provoking. Whatever your experience, trust the process and trust yourself. Only you know who you truly are.

You may want to adjust some of your temporary qualities to fit this structure in order to keep them on your list. For example, the word "funny" may convert to something more like "good-natured" or "accepting." You may also find that some of your words overlap. For example, "loving" and "compassionate" might mean the same thing to you. Simply pick the words that resonate most with your Soul—or make a word of your own creation. Continue to combine and simplify your words until you have a final list of **three to five** traits that you believe represent your authentic wildness.

These three to five traits provide a microcosm of your authentic wildness. They are not meant to be the end-all-be-all of who you are. Remember, this exercise is merely a starting place. As you become more intimate with your Fearless Soul, your list of traits will likely change, gaining clarity until it solidifies.

An Alternate Route

Some people have trouble beginning their authentic wildness lists. Others simply want to move forward and not spend time creating this list at all. If either of these is true for you, there is an alternate route.

Richard Schwartz, Ph.D., who pioneered the Internal Family Systems model of therapy, describes compassion and curiosity as the key indicators of what he calls the authentic Self[2] (13). We can feel other emotions in addition to compassion and curiosity—you don't have to be a monk—but if those two qualities are not present, it is a clear indicator that you are not being truly yourself. If you are having trouble compiling your own list, you

---

[2] During my Return phase, as described in the Preface of this book, Schwartz's philosophy of Self was my primary tool for returning to authentic wildness. I hadn't conceived of my three to five traits yet, and couldn't see who I truly was through the remnants of my traumatic childhood. I found his concept of Authentic Self simple enough to use consistently, but challenging enough to keep me engaged with the process, which is why I list it as a viable alternate.

can use compassion and curiosity as stand-in qualities until you come up with your own list.

Rooting Your Authentic Wildness

Towering redwoods stretch into the sky as tall as buildings. Their roots, the part we cannot see, spread into the soil like veins, providing the anchor to support enormous heights. Their root is their foundation: it stabilizes and grounds and allows nourishment to spread through the body of the tree. We often neglect to fill our lives with circumstances and people that actually stabilize and ground us, that allow nourishment to spread through our body and Soul. We instead opt for the spiritual fast food of television, shallow relationships, and unfulfilling work. Like a redwood planted in a small pot, our Souls become thirsty for wildness and starved for a deep foundation.

Look again at your list of qualities, whether you have a full, authentic wildness list or are using compassion and curiosity for now. Think about what activities give you the *experience* of these qualities. In other words, what activities give you the best return on your time investment in terms of filling up your authentic wildness?

Perhaps you feel your authentic wildness when you have time alone to ponder, see your favorite band play, cook a delicious meal for your friends, write a screenplay, work with clay, write computer code, paint galaxies, snuggle with your animals, learn something academic, or read poetry. The activity you are looking for doesn't need to include every single one of your authentic wildness traits; it only needs to make you *feel* your authentic wildness when the activity is complete. I emphasize *complete* because we rarely feel motivated ahead of time to do the things that most fill our tanks, but if we observe ourselves *afterwards* we can remember the feeling of a full authentic wildness and use that as motivation next time the activity comes up.

For example, my authentic wildness is playful, spiritual, sensual, and adventurous. What gives me the most bang for my Soul's buck is going for long, strenuous hikes in nature to places that I've never been to before. This activity gives me the feeling of my own authentic wildness. I *never* feel like going on a long hike at 6 a.m. on a Sunday morning, but when I get home, after wandering through whispering pines and luxuriating in the infinite shades of green, my Soul is so full I could burst. I have a seemingly endless supply of energy that lasts for days.

Find the activity that gives you the experience of your authentic wildness and commit to doing it every week. You may have to rearrange your life at first, coordinating kid pick-ups, neglecting weekend chores, or reorganizing your social calendar, but it will be worth it. Focusing on a solid foundation, an anchor activity that will stabilize and ground that most essential part of you, will allow the nourishment of Soul to spread to all areas of your life.

CHAPTER 2

BANISHMENT FROM WILDNESS

Banishment shapes the masks we wear.

At some point in our development we must acquire skills and traits that deviate from our authentic wildness in order to survive in the world. This process is called banishment and it has three forms: healthy, unhealthy, and unclassified.

Healthy Banishment

Banishment occurs whenever your Soul is forced to go against its authentic wildness. If you were naturally peaceful and reserved, banishment would require you to argue or fight. If you were naturally vigorous, banishment would force you to wait, be quiet, or be still. A healthy banishment process often produces positive results and occurs when the banisher acts out of love, not out of malice or fear (although it may seem that way at the time).

For instance, a mother who rebukes her naturally carefree child for playing in the street does so to protect her from harm, not to shame or abuse her free spirit. In so doing, the parent has conveyed something valuable to the child's Soul: who you are is wonderful *and should stay safe because you are too precious to loose.* This banishment helps the girl learn discernment that will keep her wildness alive, safe, and out of oncoming traffic.

In the same way, the teacher who urges a shy student to join a group activity does so to cultivate social skills so that he can continue to be a part of the learning community, not to bully or intimidate him. In so doing, the teacher has conveyed something valuable to the student's Soul: who you are is wonderful *and should be shared with others.* This banishment helps the boy decide for himself when it feels right to try something new or uncomfortable.

Banishment may also occur as we struggle to acquire new talents or skills as a natural part of the growing process. For example, you probably didn't come out of the womb being able to speak in front of large crowds. Many people break into a cold sweat just thinking about speaking to a sea of strangers! And yet, this fear can be overcome by practicing different traits and qualities that develop the ability to deliver powerful messages. We can choose to improve the skills and qualities that aren't necessarily a part of our authentic wildness as a healthy form of banishment.

Unhealthy Banishment

An unhealthy banishment process can produce varied and unpredictable results. Unhealthy banishment occurs when the banisher acts out of malice or fear, not out of love, and it can take many forms: bullying, abuse, public ridicule, abandonment, sexual trauma, neglect, or a family that doesn't accept you—to name a few. It can also take the form of behavior modifications such as being told not to feel or display fear, sadness (tears), anxiety, uncertainty, and so on. Unhealthy banishment is primarily a result of someone who has caused harm. In these cases, the message that is conveyed to the Soul is: who you are is wrong *and you deserve to be punished.* The banisher is actively trying to diminish or snuff out your authentic wildness.

We can also undergo unhealthy banishment in response to how we perceive our impact. For example, we may assume that our authentic wildness is causing harm in some way and we diminish it to protect those we love. We can also neglect to trust our authentic wildness and instead use judgment, criticism, jealousy, or hatred to feel better about ourselves. This leads to actions that are out of alignment with our Soul, which make us lean again on judgment and criticism, and the cycle continues to push us further and further away from who we really are.

Unclassified Banishment

Unclassified banishment includes those extreme circumstances that are out of anyone's control such as the death of a parent, the death of a pet, living in extremely unsafe communities, experiencing war, your own or a loved one's mental or physical illness, and so on. This type of banishment has no specific person to name as a banisher, however it is still banishment because qualities and skills need to be adopted in order to adapt to or survive the situation.

Survival Masks and Belonging

During banishment (healthy, unhealthy, or unclassified), we adopt qualities and traits that differ from our authentic wildness in order to survive, feel loved, and gain acceptance. These new traits and qualities that were once unfamiliar but have now become natural are called a survival mask. A survival mask is so named because it forms a layer of protection around our authentic wildness, helping us survive or adapt in ways that aren't central to who we are. Nature provides us with plentiful examples of this: bears grow thick fur coats that protect from winter snows, trees produce a hardy exterior of bark, and delicate turtles wear nearly un-crushable shells. Just as nature contains danger, so does the banishment process; without a survival mask, our authentic wildness could be too exposed to survive or too vulnerable to adapt.

Everybody has a survival mask because of the defining feature of humanity: we are hardwired with an inherent need to belong. To belong is to feel loved and accepted and it is precisely because of this yearning to belong that we experience deep pain when we do not feel those things.

In the late 1950's, the psychologist Harry Harlow performed experiments to understand the nature of love and attachment between a test subject (in this case baby monkeys) and a provider of nurturing, safety, and belonging (surrogate mothers made of terry cloth). His experiments were inventive, but cruel; the infant monkeys were deprived of touch and nurturing and kept in isolated chambers for weeks on end.

In one particular experiment, the mechanical surrogate mother sporadically harmed the baby by catapulting it across the room, violently shaking it, or ejecting brass spikes. After these events, the baby monkeys would immediately return to the mother and display feverish affection in order to regain her love and good graces. Harlow writes, "These infant monkeys' behaviors were not surprising. The only recourse of an injured or rebuked child (monkey or human) is to make intimate contact. . . at any cost" (9).

In other words, the baby monkeys would alter their behavior in order to earn back their place of belonging with the surrogate mother *even though she had caused harm*. What's more, when the babies were placed in social situations with other baby monkeys, they couldn't function properly. They isolated themselves from others, exhibited violent outbursts, and in some cases self-inflicted harm. It was almost as if they couldn't remember how to be monkeys.

Harlow's research methods were appalling, but his findings were revolutionary to the field of psychology as they helped draw a parallel to the pattern human beings also display when faced with adversity or exile. Just like the monkeys, when we are banished from our authentic wildness (perhaps by less violent means than catapults, spikes, and shaking), we tend to alter our natural behaviors and tendencies (our authentic wildness) in order to regain access to the good graces and nourishment that were lost. In order to survive or adapt, we put on a survival mask.

The Practice for Survival Masks

It is useful to know how your survival mask shows up because a Fearless Soul understands and loves *all* parts of who you are. You cannot love and understand all parts without the survival mask.

To recognize your survival mask, identify areas of your life dictated by the word "should." When you think, act from, or say the word "should," take notice because it is an area where you are *naturally one way and believe you should be another,* which is the very definition of a survival mask.

In healthy banishment, "shoulds" help us with personal safety or pushing our limits. As in, "I shouldn't play in the street" or "I should try to meet new people." Healthy banishment "shoulds" carry a flavor of, "Oh yeah, that thing would be good for me even though I don't really like it or it is difficult."

On the other hand, in unhealthy banishment the "should" holds more severity and harshness. These "shoulds" make you feel bad about yourself. As in, "I should be skinny," "I should make more money," "I shouldn't be such a looser," "I shouldn't be such a coward," or "I should work harder."

Unclassified banishment utilizes "shoulds" in the form of an if/then statement that is typically illogical, though terrifying and seeded deep in our psyche. This happens because unclassified banishment is usually very traumatic and has no specific banisher. In trying to understand these moments, our minds tend to create patterns and pick the only person available to blame (usually this person is you). As in, "If I could do or be X, then this terrible thing won't happen again." Survival masks created from unclassified banishment are difficult to navigate because they transmit intense emotion from the past.

There isn't anything to *do* with your survival mask. For now it is enough to be aware that a) you have a survival mask, b) it is easy to pick out because it is joined to the word "should," and c) noticing when you use "should" will limit the survival mask's power over your authentic wildness.

How Survival Masks Make Trouble

The trouble with survival masks occurs when we allow them to eclipse our authentic wildness and we lose touch with the desires and qualities that truly fulfill us. When we allow the survival mask (and all its "shoulds") to become our primary decision maker, we build relationships, careers, and hobbies that are doomed to fail because *they do not resonate with who we truly are*. When we don't know who we are, we will always be reaching for something or someone to love us, trying to fill an un-fillable hole, and searching for acceptance that we can not find outside of ourselves.

Your survival mask isn't something to get rid of completely. The survival mask is imperative to survive and adapt to novel experiences. The goal is not to remove it, but rather to decommission it as the primary driver of your life and integrate it with your authentic wildness by facing your fears.

CHAPTER 3

YOUR FEARLESS SOUL

A Fearless Soul forgives.

The Fearless Soul includes both authentic wildness and survival mask. It holds each as equally important and recognizes that we are most powerful when those two parts of us work together as a team. This can be a difficult to come to terms with because we live in a world of categorization and segregation. If something is not "this," then it must be "that." If someone belongs to "them," they cannot be "us." The idea that if you are authentic wildness, you cannot also be the survival mask simply isn't true. We are complex, multifaceted universes composed of elaborately interconnected parts. Honoring the lessons learned in banishment while moving forward with authentic wildness moves us past either/or mentality. To expand and include all parts of ourselves, the parts we are fond of and the ones we despise, is to love ourselves completely.

To expand and include requires some letting go—that is all forgiveness is. The origins of the word forgive means "to give up desire to punish" ("Forgive). As in, giving up *your* desire to punish or seek retribution. Forgiveness doesn't really take into account the other person at all. It's about *you* letting go of *them*. Letting go of things that are not really you makes room for your Fearless Soul to stretch through your heart and into the world.

It doesn't happen all at once. The way the tide slowly recedes, each wave crashing further away and revealing more of the shore—this is how the Fearless Soul emerges, not as a destination, but as a dance with mystery. Your Fearless Soul is the power and vulnerability of being true to all of you. It is the choice in each wild moment to face your fears, forgive, and love yourself gently along the way.

Facing Fear

As I mentioned in the Preface, I was a highly empathic child (able to *feel* others as if I were feeling myself). I underwent various forms of abuse that intensified this feeling ability to such a degree that I became overwhelmed and went numb. As an adult trying to heal and recover, I was prone to vivid nightmares: my subconscious' way of trying to help me let go, I believe.

I had a dream once that my fists were made of lead and I was beating my step-father (the primary abuser from childhood) mercilessly. My hands came down like hammers full of rage. In this subconscious realm, I beat him until he was covered in blood and my fingers were dripping with it. He huddled and whimpered while smug satisfaction curled my lips. When he turned to me, his face clouded and his body contorted until he became only a small boy. To my shock and horror, my little brother, whom I adored and loved beyond all measure, was now in his place. In this dream I had beaten the one thing I cared for more than myself and he was lathered in *my* anger and vengeance. He was covered in blood. I awoke in sobs.

My nightmare showed me that my Soul wasn't afraid of the things I *thought* it was: the emotional or physical pain. It wasn't even afraid of the person. In the deepest part of my heart, I was afraid that I was capable of such violence.

I tell you this dream because facing your fears isn't about doing something thrilling like jumping out of an airplane or covering yourself in spiders. That kind of fear is for the body. Facing your fears, in the context of this book, is about looking deep into the secret crevices of your heart and mind and seeing what strikes terror in your Soul. *That* is the fear to face. *That* is the fear to forgive.

Forgiveness

Forgiveness is an intimate conversation between authentic wildness and survival mask. It happens naturally, like winter snow that builds and collects until it is too heavy for the clouds to carry, and is then surrendered from the sky. You cannot force a snowstorm any more than you can force forgiveness from Soul. No one can tell you when it's right. No one can tell you when it's time. Your Soul knows when it's ready. You just have to listen.

For me, it happened very quietly on a cold winter morning, as fragile snowflakes drifted downward. I suddenly and acutely didn't want to hold hatred and anger towards my step father anymore. I wanted the poison out of my heart, so I let it melt like the snowflakes would: gently, with gratitude and grief all wrapped up into one.

Note: Not a Substitute for Therapy

It is important to mention here that the processes outlined in this chapter are meant to work with fear and forgiveness on the level of Soul, but in the course of trauma recovery it is imperative to also deal with fear and forgiveness on the level of body, emotion, and mind. There are numerous resources to help with the intense healing and recovery that follows trauma. Although that is not the purpose of this book, I have listed resources in Appendix B that were of value to me in my process. However, if you feel in anyway triggered, panicked, or that you need more help, please contact a therapist or a psychologist for assistance with your healing process.

Exercise 1: Finding Fears to Face

In Chapter One, you discovered the nature and traits of your authentic wildness. Now we will further this practice by *proactively* infusing those traits into your life. By doing this you find fears to face because you will bump up against places where your survival mask is in control.

For example, if one of your traits is playfulness, try to bring that quality to your everyday activities, like eating breakfast, driving to work, or sitting in on a horrendously boring conference call. In so doing, you will find places where you think you *shouldn't* be playful or *can't* be playful. Remember then that *should* is the bridegroom of the survival mask.

You may believe that you cannot be authentic wildness all day, every day. Perhaps your mind equates a trait of playfulness to childishness, for example, or a sensual trait to being slutty, or a trait of presence to being a freak. This is just the survival mask trying to protect you. Instead, think about what your trait means to *you* in present time. Does being playful mean feeling free, or is it a type of interaction with other? What does the quality *feel* like in your body? Clarity and specificity will help you remove the hold your survival mask has on your life and, over time, replace it with authentic wildness.

Questions for Exploration

Look at your list of authentic wildness traits. Really feel them in your bones. Listen to your breath and the strength of your body. Breathe and ask yourself:

* In what parts of my life am I not authentically wild?

* What would it look like if I were?

* What do my traits feel like in my body?

* How do I bring more of the *real me* into every day?

Exercise 2: Let Banishment Teach You Forgiveness

Have you ever had a broken heart? The grief is overwhelming. There is what feels like an actual hole in your chest. It physically aches from the loss. Whatever the cause of your broken heart, I hope it did not remain broken forever. Ideally, the pain of heartbreak taught you something about who you are, what you want, or maybe how to trust yourself. In a best-case scenario, you honored the lessons of this banishment, let the relationship go, and moved forward to love again.

Banishment hurts. No matter what type, banishment includes pain that can range anywhere from mild discomfort to Soul-wrenching. If you are naturally trusting, your banishment probably provided painful lessons in boundaries. If you are naturally discerning, your banishment probably provided painful lessons in faith. Your banishment will always provide pain that teaches you how to safely express your whole self in the world (even if the banishment itself wasn't safe). If we learn how to listen to it, it can also teach us to forgive.

Forgiveness Exercise

Sit quietly for a moment and reflect on the following questions:

* What was my banishment?

* What did I learn from it? Another way to ask this is: Who am I now that I probably wouldn't be if it hadn't happened?

* What or who do I need to forgive right now?

18

When an image, person, or memory comes to mind, inhale as much air as you can. Hold your breath and tightly clench your fists. Create as much tension in your body as possible. When it feels like too much to bear, exhale and relax your muscles. Hold your arms just in front of your body, with your palms up, and say out loud, "I forgive you, [X]. I forgive you for [Y]. I release you. I let you go."

These words are just a starting place. You will find your own. The most truthful words come when you don't think of them ahead of time, but when you open your mouth to exhale and see what is released from your Soul.

You may find that the person you need to forgive is yourself. This was the case for me: I had to really forgive myself for not getting help, staying, not doing enough, and for being afraid. It will take time and you will find crevices where hatred hides. Just repeat your words like a mantra, over and over again, as many times as it takes to feel free.

Trust yourself. Your Soul knows the answer.

What Happens When We Let Go

When you release and forgive, it gives space for divine purpose to flow, create the impact, and change your desire. The more you proactively let go and apply your authentic wildness traits, the more frequently you will be authentic wildness. The more you are authentic wildness, the more your divine purpose will flow. With all these tools in hand, you are ready to discover your divine purpose type and to wield it powerfully in the world. Now let's find out what your divine purpose type is!

CHAPTER 4

Y O U R   D I V I N E   P U R P O S E

When most of the people I work with discover their divine purpose type for the first time, they remark that it feels like a recollection or a memory. Perhaps they intuitively recognized something they were doing to help others, they could feel their positive impact, but they couldn't quite explain what it was.

Joy is a beautifully expressive woman with an easy smile, quick wit, and an adorable ability to laugh about almost anything. She worked for a global biotechnology company in a demanding and taxing environment. Coworkers regularly stopped by her office to vent or hide out in her calming refuge. Joy noticed during these interactions that people's body language shifted, their tone slowed down, and there was a felt sense of ease. Joy knew that she was creating this shift in others but she didn't exactly know how she was doing it.

After a little digging, we discovered that coworkers left her office feeling more secure, safe, and grounded and we explored the possibility that she was a Guardian, or someone who protects that which they love. There was a twinkle in her eye when I described the core of the Guardian divine purpose type: "Guardians help people remember that there is something precious and worthy about them. Guardians help people feel worthy of love." Her entire being lit up. "I've been doing that my whole life!" She exclaimed. And that was that.

This is the response some people have when they discover their divine purpose, but not everyone will leave this chapter with a clear sense of their one divine purpose type. You may find that two or three resonate with you, or that none at all so, and that is okay too. Please note the descriptions you are about to read are not meant to be absolute but general, and were written to help you identify your type. You will probably not resonate with every word in the description, and that's okay—we are too infinite and expansive to capture on just one or two pages! The following pages give you a starting place to understand the system but, in the end, the process relies on you to make the decision for yourself. Only you know who you truly are and so only you can decide what you believe your divine purpose to be.

Before we begin, look at your authentic wildness list from Chapter One. If you haven't done the exercises, I recommend that you do so now. If the exercises caused trouble, or you don't have your final list of traits, use compassion and curiosity as your traits for now. You do not need to do anything else! As you read, simply remember and hold onto the feeling and experience of your authentic wildness and it will support you finding your divine purpose. As you read the descriptions of each type, be open and listen closely for what most resonates with your Soul.

Enter the Garden

The seven types of divine purpose are part of an interconnected and self-supporting system. Each divine purpose is vital to the whole, and no one individual is more important or valuable than another; if one were missing, the entire system would collapse.

The best introduction I've found for the seven divine purpose types is the biological life cycle of a plant.

Let us begin by imagining that a seed is buried inside the earth where it lies dormant until it comes into contact with the first of the divine purpose types: the Initiator.

Initiator

Catalyst. Spark. New Beginnings.

An Initiator is the reactive agent responsible for cracking open a seed and beginning the chain reaction of a biological life cycle. In botany, this agent is typically heat or water that spurs a seedling to grow.

Initiators recognize potential, awaken that potential in others, and then inspire them to make that potential a reality.

Authentic Wildness Tendencies: Initiators feel the most alive when they're uncomfortable and the future is unknown. They tend to be fast-paced movers and shakers—not always in a physical way, but more in their perception of the world. They are constantly moving through ideas, concepts, and conversations.

Banishment & Survival Mask: Initiators possess tremendous generosity of spirit. However, when their ever-giving hearts feel threatened or afraid, they can become flaky, uncommitted, or self-absorbed. They can also form overly-stringent expectations of others. Other people tend to blame Initiators for making them feel insufficient.

<u>Fears to Face:</u> Initiators tend to avoid hopelessness and despair. They fear that if they fall into either one of these emotional pits, they may never come out again. In order to deal with these emotions in a healthy way, Initiators must stop and take stock of an experience; they must pause and explore what is hindering the expression of their Souls. This momentary stillness is difficult for most people, but for Initiators in particular stagnancy can be deeply upsetting. The most vulnerable action for an Initiator is to stop, wait, and allow the darker emotions to surface.

<u>Fearless Soul:</u> Passionate potential-seekers, Initiators move past limitations. They breathe life into people and the world around them.

Divine Purpose of Initiators

Awaken and ignite potential.
Help people face their fears and cross thresholds into the unknown.
Inspire passion and dreams.

Initiators usually identify quickly with their divine purpose, specifically the bits about passion and potential. The aliveness of others brings joy and a sense of belonging to Initiators. However, other types often pick the Initiator as a false front. If you think you may be an Initiator but aren't completely sure, think about your feelings regarding hopelessness, despair, and stagnation. If extreme displays of these emotions (such as suicide, over-medication, or long periods of grief) are upsetting on a deep and personal level, you are probably an Initiator.

Messenger

Authentic. Real. Truthsayer.

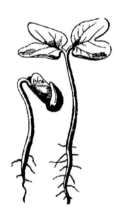

After the seed has cracked and begun its life cycle, its core stretches into a tiny sprout. Delicate, yet certain, it grows into what it was meant to be: following its truest nature.

Where there is need for honest reflection and acceptance, a Messenger senses it. Messengers remind people who they really are.

Authentic Wildness Tendencies: Messengers feel the most alive when integrity, truth, and realness are present in themselves and others. Messengers encourage others to accept reality, even if it is hard to bear. Superficiality and in-authenticity are deeply troubling to a Messenger.

Banishment & Survival Mask: Messengers possess beautifully tender hearts. When that tender heart feels threatened or afraid, however, Messengers can become harsh and insensitive. Other people may blame the words of Messengers for causing them extreme duress or pain.

<u>Fears to Face:</u> Messengers have difficulty working through the emotions of anxiety, humiliation, or disgrace. They fear their own lack of integrity may violate another, which disturbs them deeply. The most vulnerable action for a Messenger is to trust the power of their voice.

<u>Fearless Soul:</u> Honest, authentic, and real, Messengers uncover the wisdom of the heart and bring clarity to all that surrounds them.

Divine Purpose of Messengers

Encourage acceptance.
Help others strengthen their own authentic wildness.
Validate Soul wisdom.

Of all the types, Messengers are usually the most clear about their divine purpose. If you feel very clear that you are a Messenger, then you are a Messenger. If you are unsure, ask yourself: to what degree do you value truth? To what degree does in-authenticity bother you? Messengers value truth above all else, and in-authenticity feels disruptive and annoying, like nails on a chalkboard.

Believer

Builder. Healer. Fortitude.

At this point in the life cycle, the plant begins to grow. As leaves unfold and roots deepen, these extensions collect nutrients and infuse energy into the system.

Where there is need for growth, a Believer senses it and provides what is needed to make the creation a reality.

Authentic Wildness Tendencies: Believers feel the most alive when they are contributing to a cause they believe in. They have tremendous stamina and energy, especially for a calling that stirs their Souls. They understand how to cultivate progress in practical ways and how to help others through the growing pains.

Banishment & Survival Mask: Believers possess a giving heart that desires to support others in tangible ways. When that giving heart feels threatened or afraid, Believers can put on a mask of arrogance, criticism, or impenetrability. Other people may blame Believers for making them feel inadequate.

Fears to Face: Believers tend to resist grief or deep sorrow. They fear that if they enter the endless river of tears, they may never come out again. Dealing with these emotions requires letting go. Surrender is scary for most, but for Believers it can be terrifying. The most vulnerable action Believers can take is to nourish themselves and ask for help.

Fearless Soul: Wildly creative, expansive, and rooted to the earth, Believers infuse energy into those around them. They harness and direct the creative fuel for Soul.

Divine Purpose of Believers

Motivate and accelerate growth.
Help people nourish and heal.
Build the dreams of Soul.

Believers tend to identify with their divine purpose description, but they don't always relate to the name. If you prefer the idea of a "builder" or a "healer," you may be a Believer. If you find that the Believer concept is close, but doesn't seem to encapsulate all of who you know yourself to be, you are probably a Believer.

Conduit

Magnetism. Radiance. Bloom.

Our little seedling is now fully grown. A concert of blossoms unfurl, attracting pollinators and encouraging fertilization. The continuation of its lineage is now the sole longing of the plant.

Conduits sense the deep longings of the Soul and draw them to the surface so they may be fulfilled.

Authentic Wildness Tendencies: Conduits feel the most alive in moments of raw, unfiltered emotion. They are magnetic, mysteriously drawing others like the tide is drawn to the shore. Because Conduits connect intimately with the deepest desires of the Soul, shallow or surface-level desires are distressing to them.

Banishment & Survival Mask: Conduits have the heart of an artist, but when that creative expression is threatened or afraid, they can become manipulative. Other people tend to blame Conduits for their own unfulfilled desires, especially if the other person has a need for intimacy that isn't being met.

<u>Fears to Face:</u> Conduits tend to feel guilt and shame deeply and frequently, but they often do not know how to express these emotions fully. Because Conduits often receive blame from others, facing self-imposed guilt can feel unbearable. The most vulnerable action for Conduits is to clarify what *they* really desire.

<u>Fearless Soul:</u> Richly satisfying and delightful, Conduits allow people the freedom to be wild and passionate. They embody the longing of Soul.

Divine Purpose of Conduits

Evoke desire.
Help others express themselves.
Fulfill Soul longing.

Conduits typically sense that they are Conduits, but they may feel some embarrassment, guilt, or shame about it. If you are experiencing these feelings or are a little fearful of your ability to influence others, you are probably a Conduit.

Guardian

Unwavering. Fierce Love. Sanctuary.

Every biological system will protect itself. Our little metaphorical plant is no different; it develops defense mechanisms that ensure safety for the whole system.

When there is something sacred and precious, Guardians value it and do everything in their power to protect it.

Authentic Wildness Tendencies: Guardians feel the most alive when they delight in what they believe to be sacred. They help others feel intimate, present, and extremely safe, although they tend to share their deeper sides only with those they trust. Of all the types, Guardians are the most willing to sacrifice themselves for what they love.

Banishment & Survival Mask: Guardians are uncommonly kind, but there is a place in their hearts where few people enter. When that gentle place is threatened, Guardians can become physically or emotionally distant, appearing selfish or neglectful. People tend to blame Guardians for making them feel unimportant or shame them for their intense need for privacy.

<u>Fears to Face:</u> Guardians tend to shy away from the emotions of anger and rage. They fear that if they express those emotions fully, they may cause harm. It is extremely vulnerable for a Guardian to trust someone, especially if they have been hurt in the past.

<u>Fearless Soul:</u> Welcoming, stable, and safe, they cultivate feelings of value and self-worth in everyone they meet. They embody sacred love.

Divine Purpose of Guardians

Acknowledge and value what is sacred.
Help people feel worthy of love.
Love and protect.

Guardians seem to intuitively know that they are Guardians, but they sometimes feel that their divine purpose is boring. If you are feeling apathetic, or you think that your divine purpose is uninteresting, try Guardian on to see if it fits. If you think you may be a Guardian but aren't sure, think about the thing you most love in the world. Then ask yourself, "Would I be willing to die for it if it were threatened?" Your answer to this will tell you if you are a Guardian.

Seer

Be.

Plant ovules are fertilized via the flowers, and new seedlings develop with genetic variation. This new seed is neither the mother nor the child. It is something in between: a balance of the two worlds.

With compassion and presence, Seers restore balance.

<u>Authentic Wildness Tendencies:</u> Seers feel the most alive when they ride the thin space where opposite ends of a spectrum meet. They see beyond and through people, ideas, or circumstances to the context of the whole. A Seer thrives in places teeming both with life and death, places both beautiful and temporary. Unlike the other types, the Seers do not "do" anything. Instead, they are most powerful when they are completely present and fully compassionate.

<u>Banishment & Survival Mask:</u> When a Seer feels overwhelmed or trapped they can rely on tactics of control, narcissism, and even cruelty. People tend to blame Seers when they feel inauthentic.

<u>Fears to Face:</u> Seers often resist the urge to feel emotions of jealously, judgment, or hatred. These emotions reflect our own less-than-desirable qualities and most Seers prefer instead to witness the lighter side of life. The most vulnerable action for a Seer is to allow someone into their internal musings and ponderings, thus revealing how they see the world.

<u>Fearless Soul:</u> Present, compassionate, and surrendered, Seers bring relief to everyone and everything. They become one with all.

Divine Purpose of Seers

Have compassion for themselves and others.
Help others experience relief and release.
Restore balance.

Of all the types, Seers are typically the ones who think they don't have a divine purpose at all. The Seers usually say, "I don't think any of these really apply to me," or "I don't really fit." If you are feeling a lot of aversion to being typed, or you don't feel like you belong to any of the divine purpose types, you are probably a Seer. Try it on for a little while and see how it feels to you.

Converger

Wonder. Awe. Impossibility. New Reality.

Once a seed has been fertilized, an embryonic container forms around it: the shell around the acorn, for example, provides the mechanism to redistribute and replant.

A Converger brings in new perceptions that alter reality.

<u>Authentic Wildness Tendencies:</u> Convergers feel the most alive when they shift reality, creating something entirely new and previously unheard-of. They revel in the mystery, wonder, and awe of the universe.

<u>Banishment & Survival Mask:</u> Convergers possess the remarkable ability to love almost anybody. When that loving heart is threatened or afraid, however, they can appear disinterested, overly-analytical, or checked out. Convergers are often accused of being poor listeners, talking "at" people rather than with people.

<u>Fears to Face:</u> Convergers tend to avoid the feeling of being depressed or overwhelmed. These emotions can be debilitating for Convergers,

leaving them frozen. The most vulnerable action for a Converger is to stay embodied.

Fearless Soul: Connected to others and the world around them, they bring innovation, intimacy, and liberation. They become the dream-makers.

Divine Purpose of Convergers

Embrace wonder and awe.
Help others find new perspectives.
Alter reality.

Convergers typically feel resonance with almost all of the divine purpose types. They have a knack for "wearing" different divine purpose types at different times. Consequently, they often feel confused at this point in the process. If you are trying to narrow down four or more types, you are probably a Converger. If you are feeling very confused, you are definitely a Converger.

What Now?

At this point, you may still be completely unsure of your divine purpose type. On the other hand, you may be deciding between two or three types. If you are one of the lucky ones who has a strong sense of belonging to one divine purpose type, congratulations! You can turn to that chapter and begin reading now. Otherwise, proceed in one of the following ways.

If you are completely unsure, you probably need more than a brief summary to create resonance. Many people need to read an entire chapter before they think, "this is me." I recommend reading the first page or two at the beginning of each divine purpose chapter in Part II. As you read, pay attention to your gut reactions. If one intrigues you, absorb the entire chapter. Continue in this way until you have finished Part II, and then decide which type resonates with your Soul.

If you are in the second camp and are debating between multiple types, it is useful to begin with the divine purpose type that resonates most, followed by your second choice, and so on. Reading each divine purpose chapter in this order will help you absorb the information most useful to you first.

It is also common at this point to wonder if you are born with one specific divine purpose type and if your divine purpose can change. While our primary divine purpose does not tend to alter or change, it can expand to include the other gifts. It is not a static system and we are not static in it. We do change, but not linearly from one gift to another: we mature and we expand to include the other divine purpose types. For greater detail of response to these and other frequently-asked questions about the divine purpose types, please see Appendix C.

In the meantime, the most important task is to *pick one divine purpose type and try it on for a period of time.* Read the chapter, fully embrace that particular type for a while, and see how it feels to you. If it feels good, keep trying it. If it doesn't, try on another until you find the divine purpose that fits you just right.

Good luck!

PART II

Divine Purpose

Give up all the other worlds
Except the one to which you belong.
-David Whyte

Chapter 5:

INITIATOR

You awaken and ignite potential, inspiring others to cross thresholds.

"Come to the edge.
We might fall.
Come to the edge.
It's too high!
COME TO THE EDGE!
And they came
And he pushed
And they flew."
—Christopher Logue, New Numbers

Your Fearless Soul

As you cultivate your authentic wildness, face your fears, forgive, and allow your divine purpose to flow, you may notice that:

* You see the highest potential in others and ignite it, like a match to a fire.

* You can persuade people to leap off edges and try new things.

* You are adventurous, never afraid to try something once, and you revel in new situations, people, and circumstances.

* You tend toward intense emotions, physicality, or relationships.

* Whatever you do, you do it all the way; an Initiator does not hold back.

* You are high-energy by nature, and this makes you a lot of fun to be around.

* You can be confrontational without being obnoxious.

* You do not take disagreements personally. Rather, you find that when someone is brave enough to disagree with you (and vice versa), intimacy and trust are formed.

* You are powerful and present in ways that can sometimes scare the crap out of other people!

How You Impact Others
* You make people feel like anything is possible.

* You help others take risks and move forward passionately.

* You inspire self-confidence in others.

* Others find your pizzazz and zest for life contagious.

* You excite and energize people.

* People find you fascinating. They like being around you and enjoy your ability to find fun and aliveness in almost any situation.

* You restore people's faith—in themselves most of all.

Your Divine Purpose: To Initiate

In our plant metaphor, the Initiator is the reactive agent responsible for cracking open a seedling and beginning the life cycle. The divine purpose of an Initiator is the ability to shift a person, community, or organization from an old paradigm into a new one. Initiators wake people up, shake people up, and ultimately initiate them across thresholds to claim more passionate lives.

An initiation introduces a new practice or status. Its fundamental definition means, "to begin" ("Initiation"). In ancient tribal communities, initiation rituals were highly-regarded ceremonial rites of passage that moved an individual member of the tribe from one level of standing to another. The transition from boyhood to manhood, the birth and naming of a child, marriage, and death, for example, were each marked with appropriate initiation ceremonies. These ceremonies indicated that the individual had crossed from a previous paradigm (boy, womb, single, dying) into the next (man, birth, partnered, death).

Whenever an initiation occurs, a threshold is crossed. The threshold is the doorway from an old paradigm to a new one, and crossing it is often emotionally challenging and spiritually taxing. When someone crosses a threshold, they embark on an adventure into unknown realms of space, time, or the human spirit. They blossom into a new version of themselves.

In our modern era, we still participate in initiation ceremonies, though much of the spiritual and religious connotations have been lost. College graduation is a good example of a modern-day initiation. Graduation ceremonies endow students with diplomas and formally pronounce their capability to perform in a specific field of study. There are other more subtle initiations in the modern world as well. For example:

* When teenagers learn to drive, they are initiated into independence.

* When children attend school for the first time, they are initiated into a new social environment.

* When employees retire, they are initiated into a new phase of life.

* When an artist paints her first masterpiece, she is initiated into master artist status.

* When a soldier becomes a lieutenant, he is initiated into a higher rank.

In every example of initiation, a threshold is crossed and an Initiator (whether a physical person or an energetic symbol) is present. Initiators recognize potential, awaken that potential in others, and inspire others to make that potential a reality.

<u>Find What You Initiate Into</u>

Every Initiator is naturally inclined to seek out a specific potential that needs realization. For example, you may initiate new commitments or relationships. Perhaps you inspire others to new levels of courage or intimacy. Maybe you support people at the end of life, initiating them into whatever lies beyond. Perhaps you help others see the internal genius they never knew they had. Once you discover your area of initiation, you will impact others more purposefully. I cannot tell you what you initiate—only you can do that. I can, however, ask you the question that will help you unearth your divine purpose: What inspires you?

In its original form, the word inspire meant to "breathe life into." Stop for a moment and think about it. What about life, people, corporations, ideas, or technology breathes life into your bones? What inspires you in the world? When you can honestly and authentically answer this question, you will know what you initiate because the two are intrinsically connected. So take a moment and answer the question, "What inspires you?"

<u>Examples</u>

I had a friend who was bright and beautiful. She was so full of life it was contagious: she was like a walking birthday party, and everyone was always invited. It was the end of autumn when tumors the size of lemons swallowed her liver whole. The leaves had fallen away, the world was brown and dying, and my friend was dying with it. Outside, a single rose bloomed a vibrant red, fighting the winter to come: it reminded me of her.

In the spring, the fires took her body and we gathered at her favorite place. Her ashes were softer than I thought they'd be. A powder with the tiny grit of bone, they were the color of the ocean on a stormy day. How odd it was to hold a handful of dust that was my friend and also wasn't. A circle of love and loss grieved together, singing in a forest meadow. We let her ashes fall to the earth at her favorite time of day: sunrise and a new beginning for us all.

I am confident that my friend was an Initiator. Were she alive today, she would tell you so herself (with a sass and might that was all her own). In her life she created connection. In her death a space was created, a ritual that connected us deeply to each other and to the land: the two things that inspired her the most and we were all softly initiated into life without her in it.

Other examples include:

* Malala Yousafzai (Nobel Peace Prize Winner and author of I am Malala) is inspired by access to education for women and young girls. She initiates schools, programs, and organizations to empower women worldwide.

* James Cameron (director of Star Wars and Avatar) is inspired by images in his dreams. Cameron's films initiate viewers into new worlds.

* Oprah Winfrey is inspired by people who make positive changes in the world. She launches guests on her show from anonymity to fame.

Cultivating Your Divine Purpose: Get Comfortable with Discomfort

Initiation often requires crossing over a difficult threshold. For most people, leaving behind an old paradigm and stepping into a new one is an uncomfortable process. In order to enter a new phase of life, many people must deal with the darker emotions of fear, anxiety, stress, or embarrassment. If a writer wants to become an author, she must struggle through long hours, late nights, and countless revisions. Children must endure the turmoil of puberty before entering adulthood. Ending a relationship, both partners must grieve before either can truly love again.

The aim is not to make the threshold easy to cross; as an Initiator, you must accept that discomfort is a natural byproduct of your purpose. Just as it was at my friend's funeral ritual, try to hold ash in one hand and a sunrise in the other. Hold reality and possibility equally. Not knowing what is next is vulnerable for everyone, including Initiators, but this discomfort and uncertainty is where the true power of the Initiator lies.

<u>Exercise for Discomfort:</u>

1. Find a place to sit or lie down outside (if this is not possible, find a comfortable position and space inside your home).

2. Set a timer on your phone or watch for ten minutes.

3. Do nothing until the timer goes off. As an Initiator you will probably feel crazy, you may want to scratch your eyes out, scream, fidget, or give up. Don't. Just do nothing for ten minutes. Remember that it is uncertainty that brings the divine purpose of the Initiator into flow. Stay in the unknown, breathe it in, and get comfortable with it.

4. When the timer goes off, ask yourself, "What inspires me?" See what answer emerges from the space of nothing.

5. Repeat this exercise every day for thirty days. It will get easier and your answer will get clearer, you just have to practice.

Facing Your Fears: Feel the Darker Emotions

Initiators often hear from others that they are "too much." What people mean is that you are potentially:

*   Exhibiting hyper-active energy and are lacking focus

*   Falling prey to "shiny object syndrome," or

*   Have no personal boundaries around time, money, relationships or resources—you say "yes" to everything.

Typically, these pitfalls occur for Initiators when they are avoiding darker emotions such as despair, sadness, or hopelessness and focusing only on hope and possibility for the future. These emotions exist for very powerful and purposeful reasons. Some show you what is not tolerable in your Soul, others show you what you're afraid of. Initiators may fear that if they enter those dark caverns of the heart, they will never come out again.

You may avoid the vulnerability of these darker emotions because you fear (or may have been told) that you are "too much." However, when you do express the vast and rich range of your expression and emotions (both light and dark), others begin to trust you, they will be more willing to accept your help in crossing their own thresholds, and your Fearless Soul will have more room to powerfully impact those around you.

<u>Questions to Ask the Darker Emotions</u>
* Who or what has made me feel hopeless? Can I forgive them?

* Who or what has made me feel that I am "too much"? Can I forgive them?

* What parts of my life are no longer full of life? How can I let them go?

* Do I need to forgive myself for anything? If so, what?

Inspiring Initiates

Initiators inspire, it's what you do! The interesting thing about your divine purpose is that you cannot simply decide to be inspiring. You cannot say to yourself, "I will inspire these people today," and it will be so. Inspiration is a two-fold process where you first recognize those whom you initiate and, second, draw out what is inspiring to their Soul. The third and final step where they cross their threshold will then happen naturally and of its own accord.

Recognizing Initiates

In an Initiator's system, dormant potential within another (and sometimes within themselves) feels grating on an emotional or physical level. Like a searchlight, the divine purpose of the Initiator sweeps the landscape until it recognizes a seedling that is ready to be cracked. You will viscerally feel or intuit when someone or something is ready to cross a threshold. It could be that you feel chills, tingling, dense pressure, excitement, happiness, grief, hot or cool temperature shifts, or a not entirely logical curiosity. It is important to understand that these responses are simply messages—especially if you feel frustration, annoyance, or some of the darker feelings or sensations. Your only job is to notice what you are feeling and recognize that it is message indicating that that there is an initiate in your presence.

A great place to start fine-tuning your recognition is with a simple game much like "I Spy." The difference is that you will only be "spying" for one thing, and you will be using other sensory tools besides your eyes. The objective of the game is to become actively aware of the number of people who come into your space during a day who are ready to cross a threshold. Carry a small piece of paper in your purse or wallet. Mark it with a pen, make a tiny tear, or fold each time you become cognitively aware of someone's dormant potential. You may be surprised how many people, organizations, or ideas need the power of your divine purpose.

Discovering Inspiration

To discover what inspires your initiates, try weaving the following questions into everyday conversations.

* What needs to be woken up?

* What needs to be energized?

* What inspires you?

* What do you have faith in?

* What brings you alive?

* What is intolerable?

* What is no longer serving you?

* Where are you stuck?

* What needs to be ignited in your Soul?

These questions are merely a starting place and may feel uncomfortable at first, but the more you practice, the more you will get the hang of using them seamlessly. Eventually, you will find your own versions of these questions. The main point is that in every interaction, you are looking to unearth potential. What is the potential, and what is in the way of that potential? This question should be *your* main focus.

Ella the Initiator

Ella is a bubbly Initiator who works in a social position at a local government agency. Like many Initiators, she is active, constantly on the move, and always trying new things—for instance, she recently took night classes in shadow sword dancing. When Ella and I discovered that she was an Initiator, we realized that she was already initiating people in her vicinity. In other words, she was already living out her divine purpose. All she needed was the finesse that comes from recognizing initiates and discovering what inspires them.

Now, Ella says, she looks for opportunities to initiate in every interaction with co-workers. Looking through the lens of an Initiator, Ella asks herself, "What is in the way of potential?" Her conscious awareness and use of these questions allow initiation to happen naturally.

Cultivating Authentic Wildness

As an Initiator, passion and potential move and inspire you, both emotionally and physically, to the core of your being. From your perspective, there are no blocks, no limits, and nothing to hold a vision back from bursting into reality. You crave newness, movement, new adventures, and new places.

When people invite you to do something, your automatic response is usually a heart-felt "yes!" But when the time comes to attend, you may find that you have already spent most of your energy on other activities, and you feel worn thin. When you are not clear about your personal boundaries around time, money, relationships, or resources—when you don't say "no" to the things you should—you loose precious energy and your authentic wildness can dim. Be careful about saying "yes" to everything. Sometimes you need to take care of yourself and your time, money, or personal relationships and this can help your authentic wildness flow.

Recommended Exercises for Initiators in Part III
Boundaries (page 125)
Emotional Flow (page 127)
Energy Accounting (page 129)
Red Ball (page 135)

Chapter 6

MESSENGER

Your acceptance of what is strengthens Soul alignment.

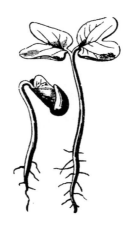

"Authenticity is a collection of choices
that we have to make every day.
It's about the choice to show up and be real.
The choice to be honest
The choice to let our true selves be seen."

—Brene Brown, The Gifts of Imperfection

Align with Soul

In our plant metaphor, Messengers represent new roots that hold a seedling firmly in place and the first stem that peeks above the earth's skin. There is a tentative moment of uncertainty when those shoots first break into the light above and dark below, but when our seedling sprouts it cannot be anything other than what it is. If it is a sunflower, it does not grow into a bean plant no matter how badly it wants to. It becomes what it was meant to be, following its truest nature. In the same way, Messengers encourage us to follow our truest nature, strengthening alignment with our Soul.

Inauthentic or dishonest behavior is deeply upsetting and almost painful to most Messengers. They intuitively sense when people aren't being honest with themselves. Everybody knows people who weren't honest with themselves: the friend who stayed in a relationship that was bad for her, the sibling who worked a job he didn't like, or the parents who convinced themselves they were happy together just the way things were. In these situations, a Messenger may ask the friend what's really going on beneath the relationship's façade and encourages him toward passion, or compels the sibling to face the truth of his terrible job while gently recalling his childhood dreams, or admits to the parents her understanding of their relationship while softly reminding them it's okay to find happiness, even if it isn't with each other.

The role of the Messenger is to help others accept the current situation, as it is—not to stay in it forever, but in order to encourage actions that will bring one into alignment with Soul.

Your Fearless Soul

As you cultivate your authentic wildness, face your fears, forgive, and allow your divine purpose to flow, you may notice that:

*   You feel your experiences deeply, although sharing them may still be vulnerable.

*   You let your heart lead you and are very brave.

*   You do not shy away from hard truths or darker emotions.

*   You prefer intimate conversations, connections, and relationships.

* The world of pretense, social niceties, and "little white lies" is difficult for you.

* You value authenticity and honesty, and the people you allow into your inner circles must have these qualities.

* People do not often get away with lying to you, but if they do, it feels like betrayal and can be difficult to forgive.

* People often thank you for giving it to them straight.

* People may be a little afraid of your forthrightness at first, but they eventually come to believe what you have to say and easily trust your word.

* You help others face truths they may be avoiding.

* You help others feel clear and aligned with their true nature.

Your Divine Purpose: Voicing Soul Messages

The divine purpose of a Messenger is to voice truth that resonates with Soul. These sacred truths strike a fundamental chord within; a place where you instinctually know the truth that rings in *your* bones. It may not be someone else's truth, it may not be a universal truth, but it is the truth of *your* Soul.

I am a sensitive creature. I live raw and exposed so that I may truly live. The trauma of my past lends my tender heart to days where my childhood surfaces for no apparent reason. I am overwhelmed and have to call in sick, or sit by the creek near my office and cry until I am able to function. There's no rhyme or reason to it, a random memory is triggered and I have to feel my way through in order to return to normalcy.

It may sound odd, but in these moments of despair, I find myself singing the various melodies of the song *Hallelujah*.[3] Particularly the verse: "It's not a cry that you hear at night, it's not somebody who's seen the light, it's a cold and it's a broken Hallelujah." The song strikes a chord within, conveying a deep truth of *my* Soul: that god is in everything, including that which does not feel good. God is in the billions of stars as well as in the

---

[3] *Hallelujah* was originally written and released by recording artist Leonard Cohen in 1984. Jeff Buckley recorded the more popular and recognizable version of the song for his 1994 album *Grace*.

infinite darkness that holds them. God is in the healthy body and in the virus that consumes it. God is in the tiny snail heaving its way across my walk and in the unpleasant slime it leaves behind. God is in my joy and in my despair.

When I sing *Hallelujah,* it isn't so much that I am saying, "Thank you, strange deity, for this awesome panic attack. I simply love when I can't function." Instead it is more a way for me to voice the truth of my Soul, "I feel you within me and I know that I am alive." The truth of my Soul is that if I go deep enough within each star, each sickness, each snail, and each despairing moment, it allows me to feel god within. It is not about what I'm feeling or experiencing as much as how deeply I am feeling or experiencing it.

This may not be your truth. It may not resonate with you at all, and that's okay. It simply means that my truth is not resonant with *your* truth. The important thing is to find out what your truth, the message of your Soul, is and to share it as much as possible. Your message will be as unique as you are and I cannot tell you what your exact message is; only you can do that. I can, however, provide an exercise to help you discover it.

Exercise to Discover Your Soul Message
Start by placing your hand on top of your heart. Take a few moments to feel your heart beating. Notice the rhythm of it. Notice the rhythm of your breath. Take six deep breaths, inhaling and exhaling to the fullest capacity of your lungs. Keep your attention on this breath.

After the sixth exhale, ask yourself: What is the truth of my Soul?

Some Messengers prefer the question: What is my message?

Whatever question you decide to ask, trust the answer that comes from your heart. The heart is the power center for Messengers; it has all the information you need to know. Trust it. Trust yourself.

If the above question is giving you some trouble, repeat the exercise. This time, however, ask yourself, "What do I resist?" Listen thoughtfully; sometimes what you resist will also point you to your message.

Some examples of Messengers and their Soul message include:
* Desmond Tutu, African bishop and opponent of apartheid, advocates a message of racial equality.

* Brene Brown is a research professor at the University of Houston. Her work revolves around researching, studying, and voicing the impacts of vulnerability, courage, worthiness, and shame.

54

* The film *Chasing Ice* (2012) chronicles the journey of James Balog (photographer) and his team to capture successive images of rapidly melting glaciers around the globe. The film gives voice to the urgency and real-time impacts of climate change.

* Mark Nepo and *The Book of Awakening* provides daily messages of hope, presence, and acceptance.

Cultivating Your Divine Purpose: Delivering Your Message with Grace

The people who really need your gift *want* your honesty. They want to hear the truth, even if it is hard to hear. It is the *reception* of a message that nourishes a Messenger, not merely the telling. However, it requires a few extra skills and a dash of finesse to deliver your message in a way that others will receive well. Below are a few useful techniques to help you on your way.

To Whom You Voice Your Message: Use Body Indicators

A Messenger must learn when to deliver a message so that it will have the maximum impact. When someone is ready to receive the truth of your Soul, you will experience a visceral resonance, a physical indicator in your body. This can show up in a variety of ways: tingling, expansive breath, intense emotion, a gut feeling, or a change in temperature, for instance. Each Messenger has a unique body indicator, but the more you notice and familiarize yourself with them, the more success you will have in delivering your message

Whenever you experience your body indicator, it is time to deliver your message. However, it is useful to employ a cross check within yourself first. Ask, "Is this person ready for my message?" Trust the answer that comes, follow it, and try to not be attached to the outcome.

Connect Intimately First

If your body indicator has been activated and you feel someone is ready to hear your message, it is important to connect intimately *before* speaking the truth. In order for someone to really hear you, they need to develop trust. Trust requires time, patience, and vulnerability on your part. Try cultivating intimacy by asking questions of the other person, such as:

* What is true for you?

* What are you resisting?

* What makes you feel most like yourself?

* What does your heart have to say?

* What is out of alignment?

* What must be acknowledged or accepted?

* What are you afraid of?

You cannot expect others to be present, open, or vulnerable with you if you are not exhibiting the same qualities so you may need to answer the questions yourself first, before asking another to answer them. For example, you could say, "I think what is true for me in my life right now is that I feel adrift and lost, although I seem to have faith that it will all work out. What is true for you right now?" You could share anything from your deepest passion in life to what you thought about on your morning walk. It doesn't matter what you share as long as it is personal and meaningful to you.

While these questions are designed to deepen a relationship or conversation, there is a version of them that is all your own and will feel more comfortable to you. The ones listed here are merely a starting place.

Word Your Message Kindly: The Marshmallow Approach

Delivering your message isn't always a smooth process. Your words may have caused extreme pain and sorrow in the past. Your goal is not to make people feel better; it is to help them be honest with themselves. However, the more kindly you word your message, the better luck you will have. You don't have to alter your message, but padding it with encouraging words will help the truth go down easier. I call this "The Marshmallow Approach."

The statement "you aren't being authentic" sounds pretty harsh, right? Even though it may be true, it is hard to swallow. To lighten the load, try padding it with encouragement.

Marshmallow: "I care about you and want to see you happy."

Message: "I don't think you are being totally authentic in this situation."

Marshmallow: "I'd love to see you be authentic because your real self is so powerful!"

56

You can put almost anything between marshmallows, and it will taste better. The same is true for difficult truths.

Sometimes the Truth Hurts

It is the nature of Messengers to speak the truth, bringing others into intimate relationships with their own authentic selves. Messengers hold up a mirror, showing people who they really are, and this can be a painful experience. People may feel all kinds of emotional responses: anger, blame, shame, discouragement, etc.

The important thing to remember is that these emotional responses are not your fault. In fact, it isn't even about you! Unless you are being unkind, the emotional response merely indicates how the other person feels about himself or herself. For example, if someone responds to your message with blame and anger, they most likely feel blame and anger toward themselves in relation to what you have shared. Instead of becoming defensive, ask yourself, "Why do they feel that way?" The more curious you are about their response, the more luck you will have in helping them accept who they really are and what is out of alignment with their Soul.

Trust Your Body Indicator, Your Message, and Your Voice

Belle is a Messenger who fell in love with a married man. Although he kept the truth of his marriage hidden, she knew something wasn't right. Her body physically responded to his dishonesty: the visceral response in his presence was so strong that she actually had heart palpitations. It wasn't until after the relationship ended that she discovered the truth—and learned to trust her own responses.

Thanks to Belle's unfortunate dating experience, she has learned to express her divine purpose in the workforce. Belle's role is to vet high-level managers for global corporations. When a candidate does not respond to interview questions authentically, Belle senses it. She knows her indicators and trusts them, even when there is no hard evidence to back them up. She has said that, on more than one occasion, her intuition about potential candidates has proved to be correct. Her hiring choices tend to align perfectly with what will benefit all parties involved.

Trust yourself, dear Messenger. The truth of your Soul will not lead you astray.

Cultivating Authentic Wildness: Free Your Voice

As a Messenger, you have a tendency to question the power of your own voice. You may wonder if you have anything worthwhile to say, if anyone will listen to you, or if they will think you a fool. The truth is, you do have a message to tell, and the world needs to hear it! It is important to connect with your message as intimately as possible, as often as possible.

One way to do this is what Julia Cameron, author of *The Artist's Way*, calls "Artists Pages." Cameron recommends that you complete three pages of writing, about whatever you want, every day. The first page is usually a random dump of worry, tasks, and other non-essentials that clog your brain. On the next pages, what starts to shine through is the subtle truth of your Soul. Notice where this voice comes from in your body. Listen for the message that comes with frequency and power, and trust it.

Another suggestion is to try singing or talking in the shower. Turn off the lights. Complete darkness can feel secure—but don't hurt yourself! Light a candle or bring a small lamp if you need it. Climb into the shower, open your mouth, and see what comes out. You may be surprised what your voice has to say.

Your voice doesn't have to be the use of words, written or otherwise. Your voice could be film, photography, graphic design, movement, gardening, political activism, or a myriad other activities. What is important is to find the conveyance system that best expresses your message. That is what I mean by voice. In what ways do you reveal your Soul to the world? That is the voice to cultivate and grow wild in. That is the voice to free.

Face Your Fears: Acceptance and Disgrace

When a person, idea, or organization is not embodying their truth, it is aggravating to a Messenger in a way that the rest of us can't quite understand. In a Messenger's system, lack of alignment with Soul in others is distracting, disorienting, and energetically "loud," like nails on a chalkboard. Because Messengers feel so strongly about authenticity in others, they tend to feel intense shame and guilt when they display varying states of dishonesty.

While Messengers are adept at seeing what is true for others, they may not always acknowledge the truth about their own behavioral patterns, beliefs, expectations, or assumptions. Accepting the less-than-perfect parts of themselves can be very difficult for Messengers. The fear of admission can be overwhelming.

Fear not, dear Messenger, there is a quick route to identify what you need to accept. To discover what you need to accept, identify what you resist. When you ask most people, "What are you resisting?" they intuitively and almost immediately respond with answers like, "I need to rest" or "I need to forgive" or "I need to believe in myself." Each response is about accepting what is: the body is tired, the heart is bitter, or a dream needs building. Each offers insight into what is in and what is out of alignment with Soul.

Sometimes the answers are darker: "I am resisting frustration" or "I am resisting grief." These darker responses are perfectly okay as well, they too are pointing towards what needs to be accepted. Many Messengers have trouble accepting the darker parts of themselves because they fear feelings of humiliation and disgrace. Humiliation and disgrace means different things to different people, but for a Messenger it means the discomfort and frustration that accompany the desire to alter present circumstances or alter who they really are. In other words: not accepting what is.

When Messengers are not honest with themselves, they may:

* Have too many personal boundaries or none at all.

* Get overly attached to the outcome.

* Reveal the truth in a harsh or demeaning manner.

* Appear invulnerable or impenetrable.

* Take themselves too seriously.

* Have no place to feel held, safe, and free.

The divine purpose of the Messenger will flow through you whether you are completely in alignment with your Soul or not. It will flow through you whether you accept all parts of yourself (the good, the bad, and the ugly) or not. However, the more you learn to accept yourself and what is present, the less likely you are to get stuck. When others see you living the truth of your Soul, and accepting all parts of yourself in a healthy way, they will be more willing to receive your message. You will have more room to powerfully impact those around you.

<u>Exercise for Alignment</u>

Kris is a lighthearted Messenger with a gorgeous talent for words and an enormous sense of love for the world. Her experience of connection is that she throws her heart over the line and prays that it lands well on the receiving end. This is how most Messengers experience connection with others. Either their whole hearts are in it, or not at all. However, there is a better way. You can root into the truth of who you are and *then* throw your heart into the world. Both are true and possible through the power of alignment.

Stand with your knees slightly bent. Rock forward and back slightly until you find the balance between. Then rock left to right slightly until you feel the center. Keep rocking left and right, forward and back, until you feel the center of all these movements. When you have found the immoveable center stand there for a moment. Feel the power of it. This is how total alignment feels in the body. From this place, share your heart and your truth. From the place of total alignment, keep throwing your heart out into the world, while staying firmly rooted in who you are.

<u>Questions for Facing Your Fears</u>
* What are you resisting?

* Can you accept that which you resist? If not, what do you need in order to do so?

* What or who has discredited, degraded, or disgraced you?

* Can you forgive them? If not, what do you need to do so?

* Have you acted dishonorably or out of integrity?

* Can you forgive yourself for these actions? If not, what do you need in order to do so?

A Powerful Message Delivered

In the 1930's, starvation, putrid living conditions, breadlines, and back-breaking work were standard for the men, women, and children enduring the Great Depression. Compelled by the overwhelming human anguish and suffering of the era, Dorothea Lange, a young, successful portrait photographer, picked up her camera and set out to capture the essence of the circumstances. Unlike other photographers, Lang intimately connected with her subjects before photographing them. She often asked personal questions about their situations, writing them in her notebook. She would silently walk through their living spaces until they felt comfortable enough to let her photograph them.

In one camp, a 32-year-old mother of seven sat staring idly into the distance. She and her children were slowly dying of starvation. Lang connected with the woman and displayed her tragic circumstances in one of the most recognizable photographs of its time. It was titled *Migrant Mother* ("Dorothea Lang"). She released her photos to the *San Francisco News*, and they created such a stir that the government rushed thousands of pounds of food to the camps and the stranded families.

In her studio, Lang hung this quote from the English philosopher Francis Bacon on the wall:

"The contemplation of things as they are
without error or confusion
without substitution or imposture
is in itself a nobler thing
than a whole harvest of invention."

It remained on her wall for years, serving as a reminder that the most important thing she could offer the world was the intimate truth of hardship—even if the reality was hard to face.

Recommended Exercises for Messengers in Part III
Energy Accounting (page 129)
Get Present (page 131)
Play (page 133)
Red Ball (page 135)
Surrender, Continued Practice (page 137)
Spend Time in Nature (page 139)

Chapter 7

BELIEVER

Your belief motivates and accelerates growth by focusing on the blueprint.

"The whole difference between
construction and creation is exactly this:
that a thing constructed can only be loved
after it is constructed;
but a thing created
is loved before it exists."
G.K. Chesterson

Your Fearless Soul

As you cultivate your authentic wildness, face your fears, forgive, and allow your divine purpose to flow, you may notice that:

* You possess remarkable stamina and dedication and can complete long and difficult tasks.

* You directly perceive what is necessary for growth.

* You yearn to see transformation in those around you.

* You may be a gifted healer or nurturer.

* You are capable of leading the way for others, and people tend to trust, follow, and listen to you.

* You likely lead a full and intense day-to-day life.

* You are happiest when you feel useful and helpful to others.

* You can sometimes overwhelm other people.

* You help others feel motivated and capable, and you empower them to embrace their own growth.

* People experience opportunity and acceleration around you.

* People are greatly impacted by your presence, even if you are shy and quiet.

* People often thank you for believing in them or say things like, "I couldn't have done it without you!"

Believers Build the Dreams of Soul

In the Believer stage from our garden metaphor, the plant begins to expand exponentially. Branches and leaves unfurl like fingers reaching towards heaven. Roots deepen into the soil, seeking stabilization and hydration. The entire plant grows into a marvelous wonder: as if the dream of its Soul were finally fulfilled. Believers motivate and encourage a person, community, or organization to develop into its fullest expression. They infuse energy into any vision, helping it magnify, mature, and manifest.

All Believers intuitively sense what we will call the "blueprint." The blueprint is like DNA: it contains the instructions necessary for creation.

Everything in the natural world carries a blueprint. An acorn carries the plans to become an oak tree, a caterpillar carries the design that will transform it into a butterfly, and a baby horse carries all the genetic information it needs to begin walking and eating almost immediately after birth.

The amazing gift of Believers is that they can access this blueprint; they can see the completed picture, the final product, or the ultimate design. Not only do they see the blueprint, they also know how to achieve that final creation. They see what tasks need to be done and in what order. Believers desire to *ground* what they grow—to make growth achievable for others. Like roots that secure a seedling in the earth, a Believer enables and secures growth by making progress practical for others.

Building and creating is what fuels a Believer; their very heart longs for growth and expansion. You may feel the urge to progress as an individual, developing your talents as an athlete or a musician. You may be drawn to a particular artistic style, cultural appreciation, or social cause. You may seek to expand and grow a corporation, invention, or idea. Whatever this looks like for you, the point is that something is growing and just by being you, you help it grow.

Your Divine Purpose: To Believe

The origin of the word "belief" stems from Germanic roots that mean "to hold dear" or "to love" ("Belief"). Without love or affection, the achievements of a Believer remain inauthentic and unsustainable. Believers accomplish amazing growth through the power of their belief. This is a vulnerable choice for most Believers, however, because believing is a loving act. To believe in something is intensely personal and private, and Believers do not give their belief away easily.

To believe in something is to actively operate under the assumption that *what you believe is inherently true unless proven otherwise*. In other words, when you choose to believe in something completely, your actions must reflect that belief.

Here's what I mean: Warren is a gentle giant, filling every room with his stature but also with his good nature and likeable disposition. Warren is the kind of guy that everybody likes. People just seem to gravitate toward him. I once asked Warren, "What do you believe in?" There was a slight moment of hesitant silence before he answered, "I believe in the goodness of people."

65

This may seem like a cliché answer, but it's true. Warren naturally assumes that people are good, and he treats them as such until they prove him wrong. This is why people like him so much. It is this action of belief that makes people *want* to be good around Warren. He believes in their goodness; therefore, goodness grows in others. When your action reflects your belief, your divine purpose becomes powerful and palpable.

Even if you don't voice your encouragement, people can viscerally sense when you believe in them. They feel nourished by your confidence in the dream of their Soul. Whenever you become discouraged, or you question your ability to help another person, remember that you *are* helping simply by believing in them. The changes may be subtle, but they are real.

An Example of Believing

By the middle of the twentieth century, there remained extreme hardships for the African-American community in the United States. Slavery had been abolished with the Emancipation Proclamation of 1863 and new rights granted, but Jim Crow laws kept a majority of the population in poverty and segregation. It wasn't until the African-American civil rights movement of the mid-1950's and into the 1960's that the dream of equality finally began to take shape and an era of civil action ensued.

Every individual who participated in the civil rights movement wasn't a Believer, but the movement itself is a striking example of Believer energy because, although the Emancipation Proclamation was imperative, it wasn't enough for the one law to proclaim "we're different now" and not be followed by action. The African-American civil rights movement spanned decades and included millions of supporters and thousands of sit-in's, boycotts, and protests. Thousands of daily choices were made by thousands of people: the choice to stay on a bus, to sit in a restaurant where you weren't welcome, to speak kindly to a neighbor of a different color. Sometimes it didn't seem like anything good was happening at all, but equality was taking root and it was growing.

For the movement to succeed, it required a wide-reaching shift in perspective and morality on a social and cultural level, but it was really the collective and concerted efforts of each participating person, one at a time, day after day, that significantly altered the course of history. It was those day-to-day decisions that brought the Emancipation Proclamation to its intended result ("American").

Believers believe in something with their whole body and Soul, and then act accordingly with *gradual*, sometimes imperceptible changes until,

66

over time, the blueprint becomes reality. It is like seeing construction plans for a city before the city is built. In construction plans, everything is laid out, drawn up, and measured. The plans include an order of construction and detail drawings. This is what the blueprint is: a complete layout of what will be. It just needs the energy of a Believer to patiently build and create, brick by brick, until the dream of Soul is realized.

Cultivating Your Divine Purpose: Discover What You Grow

I have always been a wandering spirit. From the moment I was born until my current age, I've called twenty-nine different places home. My parents split up when I was very young. Although they always tried to do the best they could, it was best practice at the time for a child to live with one parent for 3-6 months before returning to the other. Both my parents were frequent movers, and each time I left one, I embraced the other in a new home and a new town. I would stay for a few months and then return to the other who would by then be in another new home in another new town. The benefit of such an early upbringing is that I have very little fear when it comes to change and moving on. Where most people feel sentimental for their things, I feel most at home when all that I possess fits into a suitcase. On the flip side, I have also never really put down roots or felt that I truly belonged somewhere.

As I aged, I looked for this belonging in the hearts of men. Settling into one only to flee to another to seek the promised refuge, kindness, and love. It wasn't until I lost myself completely in this endless vanishing act, when I felt completely adrift and un-tethered from the world, that a vision came. Walking through the aspens in autumn, the dream was so real that I could hear the crunch of leaves beneath my feet and the kiss of cool wind on my cheeks. A yellow canopy flamed above and a dirt path twisted itself towards the ridge. From behind me, a small child came tearing through the woods, running up the trail to a man: the heart of my heart who carried a bundle of baby in his arms. My heart was so overwhelmed with love that tears pricked my eyes.

This could never be mine, I thought, it would be take a miracle to tame my spirit into such a dream. But the dream persisted. It pervaded every corner of my Soul: giving me something to believe in, strive for, and patiently create. The fruition of this specific vision is actually not important, what is important is that it held the blueprint for the life I want to build: a life of family, a sense of home, the beauty of nature, and awe for the miracle that is life. It gave me the dream of my Soul.

Every Believer will have a unique area of development—a dream of the Soul that they feel compelled grow. It is important to discover what that specific area is for you. It could be the growth of design, mentorship, architecture, homeopathic remedies, green infrastructure, family, spirituality, or love, to name a few. I cannot tell you what dream of Soul you are here to grow. Only you can do that. I can, however, ask a question that will help you find the answer.

It is a vulnerable question, so give yourself the space to listen quietly. Step away from noise if you need to. Sit or lie down comfortably and take a few deep breaths. Now, place you hands gently over your lower abdomen.[4] Imagine a small light two inches below your belly button and two inches beneath the skin. Imagine that the light grows stronger with each inhalation. When you perceive the light is at its strongest, ask yourself this question: "What do I believe in?"

Pay attention to the whispers of your Soul and trust the very first thing that pops into your consciousness. It is imperative that you answer this question because you grow what you believe in, and you believe in what you grow. The two are interdependent and cannot be untangled. You will only believe in that dream of the Soul you are here to help make real. Only you can help build it, and so you must. That is why this dream has been given to you and you alone. When Believers learn to channel their energy into the specific area of growth that they believe in, they have a powerful ability to create real and lasting change—and to be deeply fulfilled in doing so.

Some examples include:

* Mahatma Gandhi (1869–1948), the Indian activist who believed in social justice. Gandhi's area of growth involved strategically implementing better laws and government for his people.

* Walt Disney (1901–1966), an American film producer who believed in the joy of imagination. His area of growth revolved around the magic of cinema.

---

[4] The "gut" is the power center for Believers; everything you need to know is in your belly. That may sound odd, but the gut is its own kind of brain. It just utilizes a different kind of intelligence: body intelligence.

* J.K. Rowling (1965–present), a British novelist who believed in the world of Harry Potter (her main character). She helped develop an entire series of books, numerous movies, and even a theme park in his name.

* Thomas Edison (1847–1931), an American inventor who believed in affordable electricity for everyone. His area of growth lay in the world of technology and invention.

Cultivating Your Divine Purpose: Motivating Others

As a Believer, your role is to accelerate growth, but it also helps if you also know how to motivate others to action in service of that growth. When you can persuade others to get on board with the dream of your Soul, they will be more motivated to support you in whatever way they can.

The power of your own conviction is what will persuade others. Martin Luther King, Jr. is a wonderful example of this role. During the African-American civil rights movement, he powerfully and passionately preached his belief in equality and justice. The measure by which he believed in this dream convinced an entire nation of its potential. You do not have to be like Martin Luther King, Jr. You don't have to get on a podium and declare, "I have a dream!" You simply have to be passionate about what you believe in. It is your love for the dream of your Soul that will inspire others to believe in it as well.

As a Believer, the building process comes effortlessly to you. This is not the case for other people. As a result of your determination and zeal, others will experience emotional reactions that are typically a result of their feeling overwhelmed. Remember that you are the Believer and the whole blueprint lies within you. Others, however, are not privy to the blueprint and typically feel overwhelmed by all that needs to be done to accomplish such a dream

When someone is feeling overwhelmed, you can help motivate them by providing actionable, bite-sized steps that yield a sense of accomplishment—such as tasks with quantifiable goals or action items that have an end date. This will shift others' experience from overwhelm to invigoration and they will be able to take on more over time. Success breeds motivation, so help others out by giving them small, achievable goals, and working your way up from there.

<u>A Word of Caution</u>
Sometimes Believers can make progress for the sake of progress. Meaning, they can move forward and build regardless of the consequences or impacts. It is helpful to know that when and if you enter this state, you may become:

* Single-minded and obsessively focused

* Overwhelmed and overworked

* Neglectful of your physical and emotional needs

* Exhausted and frustrated

* Unreasonably resentful and bitter

These internal experiences can lead to external impacts, effecting the way other people see you. When you lose touch with your beliefs, others may assume that you:

* Make progress for the sake of progress and neglect the human element

* Are a workaholic

* Have a chip on your shoulder

* Believe in something blindly

* Refuse to believe in anything, requiring extensive data before placing your faith in someone or something.

I do not tell you this to make you feel bad, but to help you notice; of all the divine purpose types, Believers run the greatest risk of losing themselves within the power of their gift. You can appear as if you are aligned and acting authentically but if you feel, or have been accused of, anything on the above lists, check in with yourself: are you acting in accordance with your beliefs?

Cultivating Authentic Wildness: Surrender and Play

As a Believer, you are a master of independence and are never afraid to complete a difficult task on your own. Dedicated and tenacious, you can handle tremendous amounts of stimulus and may continuously seek challenging situations or careers. Because you do everything with your whole heart and Soul, life can be intense. Believers are used to working very, very hard to achieve their goals. Sometimes, though, they need to take a break and surrender.

Believers can have immense difficulty with the idea of surrender because they think it means giving up. Surrender is not giving up. There simply comes a point where you're done working, and you need to sit back and watch what happens (even if it takes longer than you think). That's what surrender means: ceasing your effort, hitting the "pause" button, and waiting to see if your efforts will "work" or not. That's a hard thing to do because it can be scary! What if all your striving was for nothing?

As a Believer, you may wonder whether you are being well utilized and genuinely useful to others. When things don't go as planned, the deadline passes unmet, or the goals remain unreached, you may wonder whether you failed in some way. You can be quite hard on yourself, pushing yourself and others relentlessly—and this is not always a bad thing. The resolve of a Believer allows you to overcome limiting beliefs and create marvels. But remember to be gentle with yourself, and give the space to recoup any energy that has been spent in the building process.

In this pause, it is helpful for Believers to play with the building blocks of reality—to envision what could be. This happens most effectively during times of relaxation and rejuvenation. The new routes available for growth most often present themselves when you are *not* obsessing over them. Give your body and brain a break, and allow new pathways and blueprints to unfold.

Facing Your Fears: Allow Grief to Help You

One emotion that Believers may not feel fully is grief. Grief and loss are broad terms. When I speak of them here, I am referring to circumstances of loss that are out of your personal control, such as death, trauma, environmental devastation, or war. Many Believers are quite adept at moving on from unfortunate circumstances: divorce, job loss, friendships ending, moving cities, and so on. They notoriously pulling themselves up by their own bootstraps and doing what needs to be done. What can be confusing is that they are not so adept at feeling the deeper grief of their Soul: really *feeling* the sorrow of the loss instead of just pushing through it.

As a Believer, you may fear that if you enter that river of seemingly endless grief, you will never come out again, but it's important for you not to shy away from these feelings. It will be more difficult to help others build and grow when you are harboring unacknowledged grief. Grief is an emotion of release, it helps you surrender and let go. When we allow ourselves to feel the sorrow of Soul deeply, it can be immensely restorative and rejuvenating.

<u>Questions for Grief</u>
* Is there any bitterness or resentment that you are holding onto?

* Can you forgive the cause of that bitterness or resentment? If not, what do you need to do so?

* What or whom has been lost to you? In what ways can you honor this loss?

Facing Your Fears: Ask for Help

The first time I asked for help was at an advocacy center for sexual assault victims. I sat in the parking lot for over an hour, going back and forth in my mind about walking in the doors. I was mortified, because even being in front of the building was an admission that I had been sexually attacked. I didn't want to face the shame or the grief that would accompany that admission. I forced myself to focus on one step at a time until I reached the door. I doubled over, the overwhelming urge to vomit pervading my throat and eardrums. From behind the front desk, a woman emerged. She wrapped her arms around my shoulders and asked, ever so gently, "Do you need help?" and I told her that I did.

"What do you need help with?" She asked.

"I don't know," I replied. The tears escaped and flowed freely while I whispered, "I don't know. . . all I know is that I need help."

Asking for help is unbearably vulnerable. Especially in the case of Believers, people assume you've got it all handled. Very often, you do! It actually requires a lot of trust for you to ask for what you need, but there is extreme power in your vulnerability.

The trick with asking for help is to state it simply, succinctly, and accurately. People often ask for help in roundabout and indirect ways, saying things like, "Would you mind. . ." or "I'm so busy with this, could you. . . ." We often make statements that require others to be mind readers.

Instead, try using the words, "Will you help me with. . . . "

It will feel very vulnerable, but stay with the feeling: of not having it all together, feeling unproductive, or being afraid. Be with the insecurity of not knowing how it is all going to work out and of knowing that you may not get it all done. Be with the fear that someone could say "No." Go into the unknown and see what happens when you are able to ask for support.

Your vulnerable self is your most powerful self: your vulnerability is what helps others find nourishment and healing.

Questions for Contemplation
* What do you need help with?

* Who can best support you?

* Will you ask them for help?

Recommended Exercises for Believers in Part III
Boundaries (p. 125)
Emotional Flow (try using grief in the Continued Practice) (p. 127)
Energy Accounting (including the Continued Practice) (p. 129)
Play (p. 133)
Surrender (p. 137)

CHAPTER 8

C O N D U I T

You evoke desire and help others fulfill Soul-longing.

"You do not have to be good.
You do not have to walk on your knees
For a hundred miles through the desert, repenting.
You only have to let the soft animal of your body love what it loves."
—Mary Oliver, *Wild Geese*

Conduits Channel Desire

Before the human species built cities and long stretches of road between them, before we lived in subdivisions and apartment buildings, before we purchased food from grocery stores and water in plastic bottles, we lived a nomadic life dependent on seasonal cycles. We moved, hunted, gathered, planted, and herded in rhythm with the land. The cold winter sent us into shelter to share fires and the stories of our ancestors. In spring, we emerged and planted seeds; we hunted and gathered throughout the summer; in autumn, we reaped the harvests that would keep the community alive through the next cold winter.

Our ancestors followed desire to the benefit of all. When they wanted food, they moved to better hunting ground and satisfied a deeper longing for survival. A momentary desire is nothing more than instinct, but that instinct leads us to deeper longings of Soul. The hunter-gatherer societies listened carefully to and were guided by instinct; their development into a hunter-gatherer society led to the ultimate survival of our species (Lee and Daly, 1–4).

Although this way of life has steadily declined in modern times, it remains a powerful example of the divine purpose of Conduits. A conduit is a channel through which something is conveyed. In engineering, conduits are pipes that channel resources such as water or gas. In the Fearless Soul System, Conduits channel human desires. When desire reaches the depths of Soul-longing, a Conduit senses it and evokes it to the surface of our lives. Conduits see the true desires of others and help find ways to fulfill those desires.

There are two types of desire that are important in context of the Conduit's divine purpose: momentary desires and the deep desires of the Soul, which we will call Soul-longing.

Momentary Desires

Momentary desires may include anything from a desire to vacation in Tuscany, to a desire to make a lot of money, to go to bed early, or to leave the office for a walk around the building. *Listening to and being guided by* momentary desires is very different than *satisfying* them. After all, if we acted on every whim, the world would be a messy place indeed! The important thing to understand about momentary desires is that they are instinctual and act like a compass: their role is simply to point you in a specific direction.

For example, suppose you find yourself craving chocolate ice cream. You head to the store, and there, right in the ice cream aisle, stands someone who makes your Soul sing. Whether you purchase your treat at this point is now irrelevant because a new momentary desire has surfaced: go talk to that stranger! The momentary desire for ice cream led you to a deeper and more meaningful desire: connection. Momentary desire is orientation, a gentle nudge leading to the things Soul truly longs for. What interests me—and what I hope will interest you—is what lies beyond momentary desire: what is the Soul truly longing for?

<u>Soul-Longing</u>
Soul-longings are the deep desires of Soul, recognizable as such because they are almost always accompanied by raw and unfiltered emotion. Soul-longings explain *why* you want what you want. Soul-longings extend beyond the moment into the depths of who you are. Your Soul may long for a sense of purpose, true love, meaningful friendships, or equality for all human lives. The most vulnerable experience for a Conduit is to be completely honest with the longings of your Soul.

Facing Your Fears: Forgiving Shame

"Our nocturnal meeting in dreams whispers that my heart needs to forgive yours. But, more importantly, that I need to forgive myself for the wrongs I have done you." — A love letter I never sent, 2000

Of all people, Conduits tend to experience the most shame or guilt because of their magnetism. People *respond* to you, and sometimes the effect is not what you intended. At one point in your life you may have been told that you:

* Change your mind too frequently or are "flighty"

* Care more about yourself than others

* Cause others pain

* Fail to maintain personal boundaries

* Withhold something others want from you (like dangling a carrot)

Conduits naturally evoke others' desires. At times, this occurs to such a degree that others become confused and think that *you* are what they want. The attractive nature of a Conduit can be confusing for others—and for the Conduits themselves. Because Conduit energy is so closely tied to longing and fulfillment, others may have confused your Conduit energy with sexual or romantic advances, creating circumstances of mistaken or unrequited love.

As a Conduit, you may fear that you are causing irrevocable harm by fulfilling your purpose. This is a common concern. Because you bring out what people really want, you also tend to bring out emotions *about* what they want. Some of these emotions are bound to be painful: shame, despair, hatred, or disgust. When that happens, people may blame you for their feelings. On the other hand, people may experience lighter, easier emotions, such as joy, exaltation, or relief. In this case, they may believe that you are the source of these feel-good emotions.

Think of it like a musical masterpiece or a particularly striking painting. When you listen to the notes of the melody or take in the colors on the canvas, you *feel* an urge, an emotional response, as conveyed by the art. For example, a beach landscape may reflect your desire for a more wistful, carefree time; the painting of an empty crib may reflect desire for a child; or a hopeful song may reflect desire for redemption. Like a mirror, Conduits reflect people's desires and emotions *back to them*. Conduits don't force other people to feel things they wouldn't otherwise feel; they simply draw out the desires (and subsequent emotions) already waiting deep inside others.

You reflect deeply held, secret longings of the heart. Your job as a Conduit is to help others clarify their own longings so they can fulfill them in a healthy way. This begins with addressing shame and guilt as well as forgiving and letting go of any resentment.

Questions to Help with Shame

* Who has blamed or shamed you?

* Can you forgive them? If not, what do you need in order to forgive them?

* Who have you wronged or harmed?

* Can you forgive yourself? If not, what do you need in order to forgive yourself?

Facing Your Fears: Claiming Desire

While Conduits are naturally tuned into the desires of others, their own desires are often a mystery to them. Because Conduits are so focused on what other people want, they can neglect what *they* truly want. Many Conduits have not yet learned to trust their desires and fear that their desires will lead them astray.

As a Conduit, you may fear—or have been told by others—that your desires are selfish. This isn't true! It is not wrong to want something and you can release yourself of that false guilt. It is okay to desire! In fact, it is imperative for Conduits because your power lies in the vulnerability of true Soul-longing.

Exercise to Discover Your Soul-Longing

You can do this exercise with a paper and pen or out loud to yourself, but it is important to complete it before moving on in this chapter. Take a moment to focus your mind and body. For help with this, see the Red Ball exercise in Part III (p. 135). Focus your attention on your heartbeat, take a few deep breaths, and answer this question: "What do I *really* want?"

Write your answer or say it out loud. Your first answer may be superficial. That's perfectly fine. Keep asking and answering the question (either in writing or out loud) until you experience a visceral or emotional response such as tears, chills, or a tightened throat. When you reach a visceral or emotional response, circle that desire on your list or write it down if you have been saying them out loud.

Listen closely. Trust your desire. It will not lead you astray.

Your Divine Purpose: Fulfill Soul-Longing

Every Conduit helps others recognize and fulfill a specific Soul-longing. I cannot tell you which Soul-longing belongs to you; only you can do that. I can, however, tell you that your deepest desire is intrinsically tied to the Soul-longing of others: it is what you are here to bring out, fully express, and grant permission for in the world. It is why you are here!

When you can answer the question from the previous section (What do you *really* want?) with a visceral, honest, and authentic response, *that* is the Soul-longing that you help others fulfill. If your deepest desire is freedom, then that is the Soul-longing you help fulfill. If it is security, love, generosity, or intimacy, whatever was at the bottom of your desire list is what you help others fulfill in the depths of their Soul.

For example, Lesley is a career counselor at a prestigious university nestled in the mountain pines. A student once came to Lesley struggling between two career options: dance or science. The student saw science as a way to be of service and felt guilty for wanting to pursue dance because it seemed like the selfish choice. Lesley listened patiently and then explained that the desire to serve and the desire to dance were not opposed to each other but were, in fact, one and the same. The student's attitude shifted immediately and she could feel the truth of Lesley's words: her desire to dance was her service to others. Lesley's deepest desire is to intimately connect to the world with purpose and *that* is exactly what she helps others feel. What a beautiful gift to give!

Some other examples include:

* Karla McLaren, an author and researcher who carries a deep desire for healing, awareness, and living empathically. Her work helps people understand their own emotions and use them in everyday life, thus fulfilling a Soul-longing that matches her desire.

* Bjork is an Icelandic singer whose lyrics embody the desire for sensuality. She helps others fulfill the desire to *feel* their bodies through the gorgeous music she produces.

* Salman Khan, the founder of Khan Academy, an online learning program that provides worldwide tutoring for every subject. The program began with Kahn's desire to help his niece learn calculus and grew into a means of providing free education for everyone. Kahn helps others fulfill their desire to better their lives through education.

* Mary Oliver, an American poet whose writing exudes the desire to be present with nature. She helps others fulfill their desire to cherish the beauty of simple moments.

When Conduits discover the specific Soul-longings they are compelled to awaken in the world, they have a powerful ability to create real and lasting change and to be deeply fulfilled by doing so.

Cultivating Your Divine Purpose: Wielding Momentary Desire

Just as your desire will point to the Soul-longings of others in a broad sense, it will also guide you in your day-to-day interactions. For Conduits to be effective in helping others, they must maintain a consistent, truthful, and open relationship with their own innermost desires. How can you help someone fulfill the deep longings of their Soul if you cannot do this for yourself? Momentary desire connects Conduits with what is happening right now, in this moment, with this person. Listening to your momentary desires will help you discover the deeper Soul-longing of others. Try using the following technique to direct your conversations to the depth of Soul-longing.

It's a little tricky to formulate, but once you get the hang of it, it will become automatic. Start by answering the following questions silently to yourself:

1. What is my momentary desire? *"I want. . . ."*

2. What do I really want and why? *"I really want. . . ."*

3. What is good about this person, their behavior, or the connection I am experiencing? *"I like. . . ."*

Now, to make the request, flip the order of your answers when you give your delivery:

1. Tell them what you like.

2. Tell them what you *really* want and why.

3. Frame your momentary desire as a request.

Sharing your desires (momentary or otherwise) is vulnerable, but it will increase the likelihood of continuing to deeper places of connection. For example, suppose you are in conversation with a Guardian (Guardians tend to be notoriously private). At some point, you feel a desire to hear something more intimate and real from the Guardian. You decide to answer your three questions internally and when you make your request, your conversation could look something like this:

I'm really enjoying this conversation,

It seems like there is more to you, and I want to understand who you are as a person.

Will you tell me what you are really thinking right now?

It may be, in this example, that the Guardian needs to open up about something specific; perhaps they have a sick family member or are experiencing troubles at work. Whatever the case may be, when you answer the questions internally first and then flip them in the conversation it will help create space for intimacy.

Using this method also gives you, the Conduit, a kind of relational insurance. When you explain why you want what you want with clarity, it is more difficult to misconstrue. This may save you the heartache that often results from misunderstanding.

Cultivating Your Authentic Wildness: Express Yourself

While most Conduits appear not to care what others think, they can be so deeply attuned to others' desires that they mold themselves to fit those desires. Don't. When you are free to express yourself, you empower others to express themselves, too.

Like a flower that opens to the sun, your authentic wildness is open and expressive. Letting others see the true depth of your sensuality, emotions, and desires can be vulnerable, but this is exactly how intimacy grows, and it is through intimacy that you will connect with your divine purpose in a lasting way.

Feel the depths of your Soul-longings and share them with others. The world needs to remember what it feels like to yearn for something real and meaningful. It is this longing that lets us know that we are alive. Express your desires however it comes naturally to you: music, art, poetry, technology, psychology, or teaching. Creative expression is the outlet for your authentic wildness to flow.

Recommended Exercises for Conduits in Part III
1,000 Permissions (page 123). The gateway to desire is permission. This exercise is an excellent place to start for Conduits.

Red Ball exercise (page 135) will help focus your attention on your body and sensations, which helps with confusion and projection.

Emotional Flow (page 127). Remember that emotions are a natural response to the deeply personal and intimate experience of desire. The more you learn to experience the range of your own emotions, the better you will be able to handle the emotions of others. In the Continued Practice, I recommend using guilt or shame in your conversation.

Your Fearless Soul

As you cultivate your authentic wildness, face your fears, forgive, and allow your divine purpose to flow, you may notice that:

* You see through superficial wishes to the deeper longings of the heart.

* You don't need the limelight, but when you are in it, you shine!

* You are sensual in the way you approach even the smallest things.

* You can be quite daring.

* Pleasure or enjoyment comes naturally to you.

* You attract attention sometimes without meaning to.

* You are a master of directing people or groups without their awareness.

* You are collaborative and inclusive and tend to consider the desires of the group above your own.

* For you, it's all about ensuring that everyone gets what they *really* want.

How You Impact Others
* Your presence reminds people what fulfills, embodies, and frees them.

* People find you captivating and are naturally drawn to you.

* People want to be around you; they enjoy the experience that is you!

* People often thank you for your full expression, which makes them feel free to express.

* People can find you raw, unfiltered, and perhaps a little wild— especially when you feel safe enough to express this side of you.

CHAPTER 9

GUARDIAN

You value what is sacred and do everything in your power to protect it.

Long ago, in a time before time, the earth and stars, rivers and valleys, humans and animals were all children of Great Spirit and spoke the same tongue. On a beautiful sunny day, seven sisters played in the meadows with their little brother. Little Brother pretended to be a great bear and chased the sisters round and round, growling with great pretend fangs and lunging with great pretend claws. The sisters delighted in the game, trembling with pretend fear.

Suddenly, Little Brother transformed into a real bear and began to pursue his sisters. The seven sisters became truly afraid. Their brother had grown larger than any bear they had ever seen, so huge that each girl would make only a tiny morsel for him. The girls ran faster and faster, looking for a place to hide, but they found none. They stumbled, and the bear was almost upon them! They saw his wide-open jaws full of enormous teeth. They smelled his hot breath.

The girls called upon the earth and stars, rivers and valleys to help them. "Great Spirit! Have pity; save us!" Great Spirit heard their cries. All at once, a tree stump appeared and told the sisters to climb upon him. The stump began to shake and rise, and the girls rose with it, higher and higher, until they were a thousand feet above the earth. Their brother the bear was disappointed to see his meal disappearing into the clouds. He stood upon his hind legs and dug his enormous claws into the side of the stump, trying to reach the top where his sisters lay, but it was no use. In time, he grew tired and went away.

Great Spirit saw the sisters huddled together, tired and afraid, and once more took pity on them. Deciding to keep them safe for all time, Great Spirit called the warm winds. The winds came, rocking the girls into a sweet sleep, and bore them up into the night as seven shining stars, dreaming the dream of the world to come.

—Adapted from the Kiowa legend Devil's Tower

Sacred Love

Something is sacred when it is regarded with great respect or reverence, when it is considered worthy of devotion. That is what Guardians do—devote themselves completely to causes worthy of Soul. Different than a religious or spiritual kind of sacred, Guardians look for the sacred in everyday things. They value aspects of humanity that most of us tend to overlook, and yet are collectively held most dear on the level of Soul. In big picture terms, these sacred qualities are things like innocence, playfulness, equality, freedom, truth, femininity, science, or philosophy. But Guardians also devote themselves to the protection of much more tangible items:

* Pristine and beautiful land which has been preserved

* Family or friends

* Music and art in museums and school programs

* Shelters that take in abused animals and nurse them back to heath

* Victim advocacy which fights for those who cannot fight for themselves

* Environmental laws that ensure the protection of clean water and air

Guardians hold equal measures of warrior and lover qualities. Guardians value and protect something first and foremost because they love it so completely. It is this deeper love that drives a Guardian; it is the essence of why they do what they do.

"Love" is an interesting term to define because, in the English language at least, we use the word loosely. We say, "I love chocolate," and we also say, "I love my children." Of course our love of chocolate is different from our love for our children, yet we use the same word. Other cultures have a variety of words to describe the subtleties of love. There is a word in French, for example, that conveys the heartbreaking pain of wanting someone you cannot have, or another in Arabic that describes the feeling of loving someone so much, you hope that you are the one to die first so you do not have to live without the other. The subtleties and variation of love are infinite, but in context of the Guardian divine purpose, what I mean by "love" is fierce, unconditional love.

I smoldered with unyielding anger at my mother for a long time. I blamed her, and her alone, for the men that came into our lives and abused my childhood. I pushed her away, this wild and beautiful creature, with such cruelty and hardness. She would stand firm and say, "I'm going to keep loving you. You can hate me and I'm not going anywhere. I will never stop loving you."

I don't know that my mother is a Guardian, you would have to ask her, but I know in this part of our relationship she was the embodiment of Guardian's fierce and sacred love. My bones knew, even if my brain didn't, that I could go off the deep end, lose myself completely, and my mother would still love me. We are the fortunate ones who are so lucky as to have Guardian's fierce love in our lives.

Your Divine Purpose: To Value and Protect What Is Sacred

Some plants grow spiral roots or thorns on their stems, others grow in thick groves or create a sticky substance on their leaves or branches. Every biological system will protect itself. In the Fearless Soul System, Guardians are the natural protective element. This does not necessarily require an act of physical protection. Do not think of Guardians as bodyguards. Rather, Guardians value what is sacred and give themselves completely to the task of protecting it.

You do not have to love and protect everyone or everything, but you do need to be there for those who want to receive your gift. We cannot always choose whom we love or what we value; these things seem to be inherent in our bones. But, you can decide who or what to defend and you will do this with more finesse, strength, and sustainability when you are clear about the sacred quality you value most.

In the Introduction to this book, I explained that you must ask the right questions—"Who am I, and how can I help?"—to discover your purpose. In the same way, Guardians must ask the right question to discover what they protect.

The Question to Discover What You Protect

First, take ten deep breaths that fill up your belly and exhale completely. Feel each of your toes, starting with the left pinky and working your way over to the right pinky. Wiggle your feet and feel your shoes, the carpet, or whatever texture is beneath the soles of your feet.

Now, with intention, deliberateness, and with all the quiet wisdom of Guardians, answer the following question: "What do I value most in the world?"

The answer to your question will determine what you protect. The two are linked: Guardians will only protect what they value, and they value what they protect.

Some examples include:

* Theodore Roosevelt (1858—1919): American President and naturalist who valued beautiful, pristine land. Roosevelt was the founding father of the National Parks Service, which serves to protect and maintain enormous areas of natural habitat.

* Dalit Freedom Network (DFN): an international organization that values the rights of the Indian lower class. For 3,000 years, the Dalit people of India have been considered "untouchable." As such they are deemed less than human in their society, worthy only to be slaves—to be broken and crushed. The DFN serves to protect their health, education, and future (dalitnetwork.org).

* Flagstaff, Arizona: a high-altitude mountain town whose citizens value clean air, history, and stargazing. As the town developed into a larger community, artificial light began to interfere with visibility of the stars and disrupt research at the Lowell Observatory, an astronomy research center built in the late 19th century. In 1958, Flagstaff was the first city in the world to adopt low-lighting ordinances. In a town of nearly 70,000 people, you can still see the Milky Way from your front porch!

An Alternative Route To Discover What You Protect

Not all Guardians receive a clear answer to what they value. If this is the case for you, don't worry. There is another way to discover what you protect.

Instead, you can answer the question, "What do I enjoy?"

Enjoyment is a full-body, visceral experience that makes you feel better. You know when you are enjoying something and when you are not. Following what you enjoy can lead you to whom or what you love, value, and protect.

This is what I mean: Sam is a Guardian who worked in sales all his life and hated his career choice. I asked what he enjoyed, and he replied, "Kids and mountain biking." Sam started taking high-risk inner city youth on adrenalin-inducing mountain bike rides that provided an outlet for their energy. He enjoyed his rides with the kids so much so that he started to look forward to them all week.

Through this process, Sam discovered his sacred aspect of humanity: "The kids who fall through the cracks." Sam left his career in sales and is now a high school science teacher. He loves to teach, but more importantly, teaching provides him the perfect opportunity to find the kids no one notices, the ones who fall through the cracks. He religiously stays late or tutors through lunch to help his students get passing grades, and his life is now oriented toward unconditional love, service, and protection for what he enjoys the most. It was a difficult journey to go from sales to science, but Sam persevered. He has never been happier.

When Guardians learns to focus their energies on what they value and/or enjoy, they have a remarkably powerful ability to create real and lasting change and to be deeply fulfilled in doing so.

Cultivating Your Divine Purpose: Follow Your Folly

Guardians hold others as precious things. You give people a sense of self-worth by reflecting the fragile beauty of their most sacred qualities. You remind us what is worth loving about ourselves. One way to cultivate this practice in your everyday life is to follow your folly. In each of your interactions, connections, and communications, ask yourself, "What do I value or enjoy in this moment?" Listen for the answer that arises and act upon it. This is how you protect what is sacred. You do not have to do anything, you simply have to value and enjoy and others will automatically feel a sense of security and their own worth.

For example, suppose a Guardian is talking to a Seer—a notoriously stand-off-ish divine purpose type. During the conversation, the Guardian realizes she is enjoying the strong femininity of the Seer. The action in this situation could be to verbalize this noticing. The Guardian could say to the

Seer, "You have a lovely quality to you, a softness that I noticed when we first started talking. I just wanted you to know how beautiful it is and how beautiful you are." With steady words and non-attachment, the Guardian has now conveyed to the Seer her own value as the Guardian sees it.

This is just an example, the words you use or the action you take will vary for every interaction. But what is important is that you learn what you enjoy, what interests you, what sparks your curiosity, and then take actions to deepen your relationship with that ideal, person, or quality.

Cultivating Authentic Wildness: Find Your Sanctuary

Of all the divine purpose types, Guardians are the most willing to sacrifice their lives for what they find sacred and for what they love. Nelson Mandela was a political activist during a time of intense political strife and apartheid in Johannesburg, South Africa. Mandela valued freedom and democracy, and he was willing to do almost anything to achieve equality for his people. When Mandela was on trial for his life, he spoke to the court:

"I have fought against white domination, and I have fought against black domination. I have cherished the ideal of a democratic and free society in which all persons live together in harmony and with equal opportunities. It is an ideal which I hope to live for and to achieve. But if needs be, it is an ideal for which I am prepared to die."
—Speech from the Dock, April 20th, 1964

The presiding judge, who was under enormous international pressure to preserve the defendants' lives, found Mandela guilty and sentenced him to life in prison. After 27 years he was released and devoted the remainder of his life to protecting and serving his countrymen ("Biography"). Many Guardians can (and often do) sacrifice their stability or sense of self for the sake of others. However, it is just as important to guard your wellbeing, as it is to protect the sacred qualities of others.

Sanctuary is a private, rejuvenating space where you remember what you enjoy, love, or delight in. It is where you spend time communing with and remembering your *own* sanctity. Even for the seedling of our metaphor, maintaining a fully-functioning plant in a biological life cycle requires time for rejuvenation, reflection, and stillness! Nature provides cycles of sanctuary, and Guardians must have time to refuel in order to perform their function well. Slowing down, enjoying the small things, and delighting in the moment will look different for different Guardians. The point is to connect intimately with the thing you love and protect so that you remember what you are fighting for. Whatever sanctuary looks like for you individually, remember to take some time to rejuvenate your body and Soul and replenish your stores of joy.

When others see you maintaining healthy boundaries, loving yourself, and caring for what is sacred and precious about you, they will be willing to accept your love and protection. You will have more room to powerfully impact those around you.

Face Your Fears: Let Someone In

It is difficult for Guardians to let someone or something into their internal space. There is a misconception among Guardians that they must maintain a tough exterior, keep themselves together, and move forward regardless of how they feel. A Guardian is, in fact, quite strong (physically, emotionally, or mentally), self-sufficient, and hard-working. This does not mean, however, that they do not require love and nourishment. Remember that it is okay to be vulnerable and to allow someone else to love you. It is beneficial to show your soft spots to those who are close to you and *especially* to those who represent the sacred qualities of humanity you hold most dear.

Letting others see the depths of your intensity, emotions, and intuitions is vulnerable. It is important, though, to show that you are human. Because you appear to be tough and strong, people may assume that you don't need them. People *want* to be there for you. They just don't know how. You have to show them.

Tell someone your private thoughts, fears, hopes, and dreams. When you express the vast and rich range of your fierce love with others, they will return that love to you unconditionally and trust your intentions. Letting someone in builds a relationship that will help your divine purpose flow more readily, with greater ease and potency.

Exercise to Let Someone In

Sometimes, Guardians don't know *how* to let someone in. If this is the case for you, try using the Red Ball Exercise in Part III (p. 135) to focus your attention on your heart. In short, place an imaginary red ball directly over your heartbeat, focus all your attention there for six breaths, and then open your mouth to speak. Where your attention is aimed is where you connect from; if you are focused on your heart, you will connect from the heart. It feels vulnerable to communicate this way, but remember: your vulnerable self is your most powerful self.

Face Your Fears: Claiming Anger

Many Guardians have trouble working through the emotions of anger and rage. The interesting thing about this emotional avoidance is that Guardians do not avoid anger because they fear it themselves. Rather, they avoid anger because they fear they might cause harm to others. It isn't that they necessarily fear they will hit or physically injure someone. They are more afraid that anger and rage cannot be controlled and will irrevocably damage someone they love internally. Even in their emotions, they are protecting others!

Many Guardians are quite adept at fighting injustice when it comes to others. What can be confusing is that they are not so adept at fighting injustice against themselves. They often do not know how to use anger in a healthy way, stand up for themselves, and protect their own sanctity. Learning to view yourself as valued, loved, and worthy of protection is a healing journey for most people, but for Guardians it is a lifelong lesson. This lesson begins with feeling your anger.

Of all the divine purpose types, Guardians have the most difficulty forgiving others—and forgiving themselves. As a Guardian, you have a tendency to question whether you have given enough, done enough, or been there enough for others. The root of all these fears are the questions, "Am I enough?" or, "Am I worthy?" This high expectation is the reason Guardians can protect and serve the most precious, sacred, and worthy aspects of our human existence but it is also what keeps their anger pent up.

Questions to Help with Anger or Rage
* What or who has made you feel as if you aren't enough?

* Can you forgive this person or experience?

* What or who has made you believe that you don't deserve to be loved?

* Can you forgive this person or experience?

* What sacred part of your Soul needs protecting?

* Is there something you need to forgive yourself for? What is it?

Your Fearless Soul

As you cultivate your authentic wildness, face your fears, forgive, and allow your divine purpose to flow, you may notice that:

* Others find you to be uncommonly kind.

* You can appear mysterious.

* You are uncommonly trustworthy.

* Injustice bothers you to a higher degree and you feel compelled to help in some way.

* You are deliberate and wise, and others seek out this wisdom in you.

* You don't chase the limelight; you would rather help out in tangible ways that make a difference in the real world.

* You can be intense in your interactions. Lukewarm connections bother you.

* You share your feelings because intimacy and connection are important.

* It's hard to get inside your heart, but when someone is "in," they are "in" for life.

* You provide sanctuary for others.

* You embody fierce love.

Recommended Exercises for Guardians in Part III
Boundaries (p. 127)
Emotional Flow (try using Anger in the Continued Practice) (p. 129)
Energy Accounting (p. 131)
Get Present (p. 133)

CHAPTER 10

S E E R

Your compassion restores balance.

"Without the shadow—nothing."
—Sundial inscription

Everything Is Connected

The divine purpose of a Seer is not perfect vision, as the name may imply. Rather, the Seers' gift is their ability to see *into and through* people, ideas, or circumstances to the context of the whole. When non-Seers look at their lives, they often see only the current situation. Seers look at the same situation and "step back" from it, placing it in the context of a larger story. In short, Seers provide much-needed perspective. To a Seer, no person or situation is an isolated phenomenon. Everything is connected: all parts of life are pieces of a larger story.

The conventional method of delineating constellations is to trace shapes from the stars, like a cosmic game of connect-the-dots. In Australian Aboriginal culture, however, the dark patches of sky, the space between the lights, define constellations. The murky nebula, which are clouds of dust and gas, appear as black forms against the Milky Way and define the Aboriginal constellations.

In much the same way for Seers, it is the space between that is meaningful. Seers can imagine that there are invisible chords that connect to everything: between birds in the flock, fish in the sea, and each of us to another. To a Seer, it is these connections between individuals that create the whole.

The Seer's energy channels through each of us, whether we are Seers or not. Without the energy of the Seer, the world would fall into disconnection, isolation, and such extreme forms of discord that we would forget are part of something more. We would forget what it means to belong to a story that is greater than our own—to believe in something beyond what we can see, touch, and smell. It is the energy of the Seer that keeps us in relationship with the mystery: the beautiful, mystical, otherworldly aspects of being alive.

Practice Seeing the Space Between

To practice the idea of everything being connected, take an iPod, MP3 player, CD player, or radio outside to a public place. Scroll through the music collection until you find the rhythm that most reflects the setting you are in. You will know you've found the right song because it will seem like people walk, doors slam, dogs bark, everything matches the tempo of the song. This is the music of the space between.

Your Divine Purpose: Be

From our plant metaphor, Seers represent the seed of the plant. Created after the plant has been fertilized, the seed transfers genetic material that is different from its parent to the next generation. It carries the evolutionary components necessary to ensure the survival of the biological line. The seed is life and death embodied. It is neither the old plant nor is it the new one; it exists between worlds.

The primary difference between Seers and the other divine purpose types is that there is no specific action or task for Seers to complete. Because the Seers' divine purpose requires them to *be* rather than to *do*, Seers often do not realize that they are having tremendous impact. In fact, many Seers question whether they have a divine purpose at all. The truth is, however, that the simple act of seeing profoundly alters what is being observed. This is called the "observer effect."

The observer effect refers to the changes that take place when something is being observed. A simple example is: do you act the same way in the privacy of your home as you do in front of other people? Probably not. The observation of others modifies your behavior.

This same phenomenon occurs in quantum physics. Experiments have demonstrated that a beam of electrons is influenced in direct proportion to how much it is being monitored. The observation alters the outcome of the experiment ("Nature"). Just like particles, people change when a Seer is totally present and witnessing them compassionately.[5]

The total presence of a Seer results in a distinct effect: it restores balance. In the realm of the Seers, balance means *the simultaneous existence of two extremes*. Life and death, creation and destruction, order and chaos— Seers regard and value them equally. Holding two extremes can be disorienting, but the line between opposites is the sweet spot for Seers because they understand that the world flourishes because of both. There can be no light without darkness, no kindness without harm, no healing without pain, and no belonging without isolation. That the world contains both extremes is what makes it so beautiful and painful to be alive. How would you really know you were alive if you only knew beauty, or if you only knew pain? The balance of the two is what creates life that is rich and diversified.

---

[5] From its origins, compassion means "to suffer together" (Compassion). It is the ability to "be with" others in their suffering without needing to fix it.

Cultivating Your Divine Purpose: Being Present

"How do you be present?" is a common question for those who haven't heard the term before. First, let us define presence as clarity of thought, emotion, and body. Presence is the feeling when you are experiencing what many athletes call, "the zone": everything is in flow. In presence, *there is no was; there is no will be; there is only now.*

Most Seers know this place of presence, but it is typically a state that happens of its own accord without much conscious awareness. To create presence for yourself, sit calmly wherever you are, relax your shoulders, inhale deeply, and ask, "What is here right now?" Try not to make anything up or create more than what is. Simply answer the question. Exhale deeply, let it go, and repeat, "What is here right now?"

Presence is difficult to maintain indefinitely. Life gets tough and we all need to check out of it from time to time (devouring a pint of particularly delicious ice cream is my favorite way to do this). Don't worry. Presence is a practice and it takes time to cultivate it. You don't always have to be, get more, or make others present. You get to decide for yourself when you want to be present and when you don't. You are always at choice.

Cultivating Your Divine Purpose: Find What You Balance

As a Seer, you will be drawn toward a specific spectrum in need of balance. Recognizing the spectrum that is unique to you will restore balance more quickly and with greater effectiveness simply because you are aware of it. I realize that it sounds a little out there, but you'll have to trust me for I, myself, am a Seer who has struggled to understand this phenomenon.

Every Seer has a spectrum that contains two extremes. Many Seers focus on the lighter end of their spectrum because they fear the anxiety, miscommunication, hurt feelings, and arguments that often occur at the darker end. Remember that only by acknowledging *both extremes of your unique spectrum* will you restore balance. You must be willing and able to be present with and have compassion for both.

Example I: As a Seer, my own spectrum is the extremes of beauty and pain. When I am completely present with people (which isn't all the time, but does happen) one of two things occur: either they feel totally alive and see the beauty all around them, or a deep and heart-wrenching pain surfaces. I believed the pain was my fault, that I somehow forced that darkness onto others. But I came to realize that people are just *in* pain and my witnessing allows it to surface. Compassion brings the pain into balance with beauty, and vice versa. If I cannot be with the pain in others and in myself, then balance is not restored.

Example 2: The traditional method of training horses "breaks" the animal by repeatedly beating and bullying it into submission. In the more gentle horse training method called "natural horsemanship," trainers observe the unique tendencies and needs of each horse and work to create an intimate connection. In the 2011 documentary film *Buck*, Dan "Buck" Brannaman transcended his abusive childhood by becoming a disciple of and the world's leading expert on natural horsemanship.

Buck's exceptional talent for truly seeing the essence of each horse is almost spiritual to experience. He sees the spectrum of the horse's past and future, the healed horse they could be, and the horse that has been beaten and abused. Through Buck's compassion and presence, horses that were otherwise unruly, un-trainable, or scheduled to be put down are restored to balance and completely transformed.

Example 3: Hannah is a normally quiet and shy administrative assistant in an American education company. Meetings at her workplace often erupt into disagreements. Hannah sensed lack of harmony among her coworkers. It frustrated her when they forgot the mission of the company and, in some cases, when they weren't even arguing about the same topic. For such an unassuming creature, Hannah was compelled to speak up forcefully because her whole being responded to the discord. She would blurt surprising and sometimes harsh observations that would, ultimately, bring the group into alignment.

Hannah balances connection and fragmentation. In this particular situation, restoring balance meant dissolving the argument. In another situation, however, Hannah's gift might have had the opposite effect. Sometimes anger, resentment, jealousy, or any of the other "darker" emotions are necessary to bring someone or something into balance.

Your Spectrum
The best way to discover what you balance is is to ask yourself, "What do I see?" Put another way, "What do I feel compassion for?" For you, seeing and balancing are one and the same activity. Your presence creates change. Your compassion restores balance.

99

The question, "What do I see?" or, "What do I feel compassion for?" will take time and patience to answer. To begin now, feel the sensations of your body, and then ask, "What do I see in this moment? What do I have compassion for in this moment?"

You may get a clear and accurate response right away. If you are like most Seers, however, you will need to ask these questions multiple times before answering them completely. Every time you feel connected, alive, or authentic, ask yourself, "What do I See?" or, "What do I feel compassion for?" Let the answers come from your Soul. Try to arrive at one-word answers, and then find their opposites. You are ultimately looking for a spectrum.

Cultivating Authentic Wildness: Make Space for "Nothing"

Seers are generally solitary people. Being a Seer does not necessarily equate with being an introvert, however, Seers feel energized when they connect to the deeper questions of life, which often occurs in a solitary and silent space.

Seers crave a feeling of spaciousness: of doing nothing, having nowhere to be, and nothing to accomplish. This can happen in physical space—such as mountain air or a wide-open field of grass—but also in emotional or mental space. They key ingredient here is to find a space where there is nothing to do and nowhere to be. If you have to make an appointment with yourself to do this, fine. But do it.

Our entire Western culture is based on performance and tasks, so you may feel bad about yourself when you choose to be still. Nevertheless, you must do whatever it takes to be present, compassionate, and able to witness without attachment.

As a Seer, it is important to give yourself permission to follow your bliss and take roads less traveled. Give yourself permission to play. Give yourself the space to think, ponder, and do nothing. This is where you will discover the true power of your divine purpose.

Practice for "Nothing Time"

Open up your calendar and find a forty-five minute block of time this week that you can claim for yourself. It might be during a lunch hour, early one morning before the kids wake up, or an evening when your partner is working late. Make an appointment with yourself during this block of time to "do nothing." Doing nothing could be as simple as watching leaves change outside your window, strolling around your neighborhood, knitting on your porch, or listening to music. Try to avoid technology: television, video games, Internet surfing, anything that is screen-time does not count as "nothing" because your brain is being actively stimulated by an outside source instead of an internal one. Find the time. Put it in your calendar. Commit yourself to the task of doing "nothing."

Cultivating Authentic Wildness: Ask the Big Questions

Seers are insatiably curious. In fact, sometimes when a conclusion is achieved, a Seer can feel disappointed! It is the movement *toward* the conclusion, the freedom of asking and wondering, that brings a Seer most alive. The hard-to-define, abstract questions are often more interesting to Seers than any answer could be. For example, a Seer doctor may be driven by a question like, "Why and how does a human body function?" or, "What is the nature of illness?" A Seer accountant may wonder about the nature of money, the personality of cash, or why and how the financial system operates.

Keep asking the big, tough, abstract questions. If you feel out of balance, finding the right question will move you forward. Here are a few to try:

* What would be fun?

* What would surprise me?

* What would make me feel alive?

* What is desire?

* What is surrender? What is death? How are they different?

* What am I curious about?

* What is out of balance?

* When all else fails, ask, "What is the right question to ask?"

Facing Your Fears: Make Friends With Jealousy and Hatred

Many Seers have trouble with the shadow aspects of jealousy, envy, and hatred. These emotions reflect the current state of your emotional and physical resources, revealing parts of yourself you do not accept. It is like that old saying goes: "We judge in others what we cannot accept in ourselves." You may think, "But I am not a jealous or hateful person!" That is true. While you are neither hateful nor jealous, the *emotions* of jealousy and hatred may pass through you from time to time. These emotions serve as a messaging system, showing you what you have not loved and accepted in yourself. The way to work through them is to have compassion for yourself first, and then for others.

A while ago, a friend of mine wanted to move to Hollywood and become a famous actor. I was infuriated because (I claimed) his desire was selfish. He was missing the point of his art, I said. He was being a fool. Such a negative response for someone following his dream! I finally had to ask myself why his desire to be famous *bothered* me so much. I listened to my heart and a little voice inside answered that I was jealous because part of *me* wanted to be famous. Gasp!

Jealousy is tricky in that it is a mirror. We must allow the surface response to fully express so we can dig deeper and find out what's really going on. Here's what I mean: Instead of chastising myself for the part of me that wanted to be famous, I allowed myself to *really* want fame for a while. I allowed myself to feel the hunger of it, and then I let it go. Beneath the need for fame was the desire to be seen and recognized, to have affirmation for meaningful work.

The jealousy I felt toward my friend provided an opportunity to love and accept a part of myself I didn't appreciate at first blush. When I stopped long enough to listen, I discovered that beneath the jealousy of fame was the true desire for purpose. What a gift my friend gave to me!

Questions for Working with Jealousy and Hatred

* What or whom are you jealous of? What is beneath the jealousy?

* What or whom do you hate?

* Can you forgive them? If not, what do you need in order to forgive?

* Do you love yourself completely?

* Is there something you need to forgive yourself for?

Face Your Fears: Share the Mystery

Seers feel most vulnerable when sharing their visions, imaginings, and philosophical ponderings with others. Seers will tend to reserve their perceptions, especially if they fear others may not value them. It takes an enormous amount of trust for Seers to speak, write, or communicate what they "see" and it is tremendously vulnerable. So, share yourself in whatever way feels most comfortable to you. Go into the unknown and share the mystery as you perceive it. It is what you were born to do.

Your Fearless Soul

As you cultivate your authentic wildness, face your fears, forgive, allow your divine purpose to flow, and share what you "see" with others, you may notice that::

* Others feel a sense of clarity and relief.

* People feel seen, heard, and deeply understood.

* People feel balanced or centered.

* People find you enchanting.

* People are in awe of you.

* You *evolve* people, groups, or environments to what is next.

* You feel powerful and beautiful, and others see you that way, too.

Recommended Exercises for Seers in Part III
Red Ball (p. 135): this exercise will help you focus your attention on your body and attention, which will assist you with presence. Try placing the red ball in your heart cavity and ask, "What is here now?"
Get Present (p. 131)
Play (p. 133)
Surrender (p. 137)

CHAPTER 11

C O N V E R G E R

You embrace wonder-filled realities and bring others to embrace them as well.

"We are the music makers, and we are the dreamers of dreams."
—Arthur O'Shaushnessy

Convergers Alter Reality

Have you ever read the book or watched the film *Alice in Wonderland*? Alice is an exceptionally inquisitive child with wild notions and a vivid imagination. On a lovely summer day, while reading in the fields by her home, she spies a white rabbit. A curious and odd creature, she becomes quite taken with it. The white rabbit hops down a hole, through which Alice immediately follows, dropping her into a topsy-turvy world where all of her fantastical ideas are real—and perhaps a bit frightening. Alice adventures through Wonderland until she awakes in the field by her home, realizing it was all just a dream. What an appropriate illustration of the Converger's divine purpose!

In our plant metaphor, Convergers represent the dispersing mechanism that replants and spreads seedlings into uncharted territory (e.g., fruit, gourds, pinecones). Like a fruit or gourd planted in a new soil, sprouting into a new world, the divine purpose of a Converger is to follow ideas where they lead and create new realities from them.

To a Converger, the upside down and inside out world of Wonderland is more of a home than the real world because Convergers defy assimilation or classification. Here's what I mean: when babies are born, they receive input, but none of it *means* anything. Babies don't have words or concepts for "chair" or "daddy"; rather, they *experience* objects and people as symbols, sensations, and emotions. Convergers receive data about the world around them similarly. They have the ability to see it without completely boxing it in. This allows them the freedom to be inventive, perceive complex problems, and create elegant solutions.

Most of us take our current situations for granted, assuming this is simply the way the world works. Tax laws, the quantum vacuum, time travel, unifying the government, complex musical compilations, neurological programming, most people do not spend time wondering about these areas or trying to improve them. Convergers, on the other hand, are enamored with these larger issues and are often able to formulate simple solutions by implementing new ideas, perspectives, concepts, beliefs, or systems.

The Converger's solution may not always be viable in its application at the present time. Sometimes the collective consciousness isn't equipped to handle a new idea. Still, it is often the Convergers who see the forest through the trees. Some of the greatest thinkers, inventors, and creators throughout history have been Convergers—men and women who were considered "ahead of their time." For example, Leonardo da Vinci conceived of airplanes long before the Wright brothers were born. Nikolai Tesla tinkered with wireless technology at the turn of the century, nearly 100 years before its advent. Other examples of well-known Convergers are:

* Pablo Picasso (1881–1973): Spanish painter who illustrated people's faces in a way no one ever had ever seen before. By drawing the subjects' eyes in the "wrong" spot, he was able to create two perspectives at once (profile and full-face).

* M.C. Escher (1898–1972): Dutch graphic artist most famous for his woodcuts, lithographs, wood engravings, and countless drawings and sketches. Escher toyed with mathematics and architecture by creating impossible objects. Many of his works are an exploration of infinity—never-ending patterns, continuous staircases, and tessellations. Escher deliberately pulled apart reality to help his audience visually stand in the perspective of infinity.

* Eckhart Tolle (1948–present): New York Times bestselling author of *The Power of Now* and *A New Earth*. Tolle is one of the most influential spiritual leaders of the modern era. At the age of 29, he experienced a profound inner transformation that greatly influenced his teachings. Tolle offers a new awareness steeped in the understanding of ego (mind consciousness) versus spiritual (higher consciousness) that leads us to understand ourselves in a new and more expansive way.

* Willy Wonka (fictional character): Willy Wonka is not a real person, but the manner in which he playfully invents new and wild sweets, never following logical procedures or using the same method twice, is entirely representative of the inventive and childlike spirit of a Converger. Willy Wonka's entire factory was a new reality for the children who came to visit.

Your Divine Purpose: To Converge

A convergence point is a location in space or time where multiple lines intersect. To "converge" is to actively draw lines together until they form a single point. Like Alice following the white rabbit, Convergers follow an idea into different imaginary or real scenarios. To others, it may seem like

Convergers jump randomly between unrelated topics. The truth is that Convergers aren't going on tangents at all; the topic is simply more complex than other people realize.

To a Converger, following an idea is like chasing the white rabbit through many rooms: each room the rabbit occupies gives the Converger more information about who and what that rabbit is, how it works, and how it could be useful to others. Once a Converger has followed the rabbit through all rooms, they simply gather the data and ask, "What is the point of all this?" Many Convergers report that following the white rabbit feels like collecting multiple puzzle pieces. During the moment of convergence, the moment of asking "what is the point?" those puzzle pieces suddenly snap into place and become clear all at once. This can be quite an extraordinary experience for Convergers and for the people around them.

As a Converger, you will find that making a point will help you connect with people. They will engage with you, and the brilliance of your gift will truly shine. The fascinating aspect of converging is that you don't need to explain how you reached your point. You need only make it. Then, if you have been engaged and connected with your audience, they will "get" it right away. It's an amazing process to witness!

An Example of Converging

Brian Swimme is a lively and passionate professor of cosmology, who also happens to be an extremely gifted Converger. I had the good fortune once of seeing him give a speech and it remains one of my favorite examples of a Converger in action. A grey puff of hair bounced to the rhythm of his step as he walked onstage. The moment Brian's foot touched the podium he immediately began talking about the origin of the universe. He continued through seemingly unrelated talking points: calling the quantum vacuum "infinite generosity," relating the history of astronomy and space travel, and examining the details of baking raisin bread. He paced and gesticulated, the dark fabric of his suit desperately trying to keep up with every movement.

He chased ideas for well over thirty minutes. Although each subject was pertinent, there was a moment, somewhere just after the raisin bread discussion, when the crowd started to get restless and lose interest. The confusion was palpable. If Swimme had kept going, he would have lost them completely. Instead, in that moment, he made the culminating point of his talk: that each and every human being on the planet, each and every star in the galaxy, and each and every galaxy in the entire cosmos, is *the center of the universe.*

The entire room was stunned into silent shock. The idea that *they* were the center of the universe—along with every molecule that exists in the cosmos—was a notion that completely flipped the audience members' reality upside down. Their minds were officially blown. People left the seminar in wonder and awe, and feeling that their very existence was a miracle. What a beautiful and poignant example of a Converger doing what they do best: bringing in new perceptions and altering reality.

Cultivating Your Divine Purpose: Follow This Process

People *want* to understand you and your perspective. They long for the wonder and awe that you convey, and they yearn for a taste of the infinite. The Convergers I've seen successfully fulfill that yearning follow three distinct steps. They:

1. Follow the idea

2. Stay engaged and connected with others

3. Make a point.

Let's examine each step in further detail.

Step 1: Follow the Idea

Convergers are sometimes, but not always, accused of being poor listeners. This is the most common complaint Convergers hear about themselves from others: that they "talk over" people, or don't listen. The truth is that Convergers can be excellent listeners. They simply get so interested in the topic, in the chasing of the idea, that they tend to "lose" people partway through a conversation, unintentionally excluding them from the exploration process. It is important for Convergers to recognize that they tend to lose people during this first step, however following an idea is tremendously important and should not be denied or shut down.

It will be useful to you, as a Converger, to create more of a conversation in this first step (as opposed to a monologue) by sharing things about yourself that are real, vulnerable, and interesting *to the other person*. Also, ask that those present with you provide real, vulnerable, and interesting information about themselves as well. This will create a conversation that is more like a dance that includes everyone which, ultimately, gives you adequate time and space to follow ideas. Besides, just like dancing, chasing rabbits is more fun with a partner!

Step 2: Stay Engaged and Connected with Others

One of the best examples I know of staying connected is a particular exercise used in some types of horse therapy. Horses are incredibly empathic creatures and are highly attuned to the intentions of their riders. In this particular exercise, a person stands next to the horse and creates a connection in order to achieve the goal of walking side by side to a post that is some distance off. The horse has no reigns and cannot be pushed, threatened, or bribed to move forward; the connection with the participant must be so strong that the horse *wants* to come along.

Some people get so wrapped up in the connection with the horse that they forget about the post altogether and give up walking anywhere. Most Convergers, on the other hand, get so excited about the post that they completely forget about the horse and leave the animal behind! This same behavior can occur with other human beings. In this case, the post would represent an amazing idea, infinite possibility, or cosmic awareness. Convergers often take off in a conversation or thought process and forget to include everybody else. The result is that they lose people's attention. People become confused and overwhelmed, which can lead to frustration and, sadly, dismissal.

Often you can prevent this unfortunate cycle and re-establish connection simply by slowing down and checking in. Look the other person in the eye and ask yourself, "Is this person still with me?" Be honest with yourself. Make sure others are actively engaged and not just pretending to listen. Keep in mind that if you lose your audience, the brilliance of your divine purpose will never be realized. The only way you're going to know if you've lost people is by observing them. If you haven't lost them, keep chasing your rabbit. However, if you notice that people are responding to you with confusion, are no longer paying attention to your dialogue, or have a "deer in the headlights" look, it is time to make a point.

Step 3: Make a Point

It can be easy for Convergers to simply keep chasing ideas, however, in order to shift reality, Convergers must always (always!) make a point.

Gather all of your ideas—everything you have wandered over, around, and under—and ask yourself, "What is the point of all that?" When you ask this question, it helps you converge multiple points of understanding into a solid, grounded, and present point of contact. State your point to the other person. Only then will other people connect with your ideas.

This final step is where *other people feel most connected to the Converger.* Many Convergers don't feel any different at this phase in the process, but other people feel deeply connected and powerfully impacted. If others know you are going to come back to the present moment and make a point, they are more likely to stick around while the idea is being chased. It is this final step that creates new realities for other people, helping them to open up to new ideas and shifting their perspectives. In every interaction you want to follow the ideas that come bubbling up, chase them around for a bit, but remember to stay connected to your body and to others and make a point of your wanderings! *The point is what will alter people's reality.*

Face Your Fears: Get Present

Presence refers to full-body awareness: intimate communion with both the internal and the external. As you root deeper within your body, the power of your divine purpose becomes amplified. The more grounded and present you are, the more powerful the effects of your gift will be. However, getting in the body can be a vulnerable task. Many Convergers spend a lot of time *not* in their bodies—that is, they spend much of their time in their imaginations, playing with ideas.

It can be challenging for Convergers to pay attention to their bodies. This creates a problem because, when they do finally return to the real world, the abundance of data, stimuli, and emotions can overwhelm them. Emotions and sensations have become backed up in their absence and spill out all at once. For some Convergers, this emotional overwhelm can lead to feelings of confusion, fear, and even panic. While you are not a fearful or panicked person, the *emotions* of fear and panic may pass through you from time to time. These emotions serve as a messaging system, pointing you toward anything that is overwhelming in your internal or external environment.

The trick with these kinds of emotions is to stay put in your body and not to fight them. The more present you stay, and for longer periods of time, the more you will find yourself capable of riding these emotions like great waves. You will be able to deal with them individually instead of facing a tsunami of backed-up energy.

If you find the panic or the fear to be incapacitating, please do seek professional help, as these emotions can also be signs of trauma.

Face Your Fears: You May Wonder if You Deserve To Be Loved

Of all the divine purpose types, Convergers feel the most alone. This is not the same as feeling lonely, which implies that a person is actively longing for connection with others. Rather, Convergers can hold a secret fear that they are flawed in such a fundamental way that they will never belong to the world. Internally, you can sometimes feel:

* Like an outcast or alien, as if you don't belong on the planet.

* Like there is no point to your existence.

* Frozen, numb, or unable to decide or act.

* Like you are unlovable.

It is important for Convergers to understand that being different is part of what makes your purpose so powerful. Isolation is a natural side effect of operating in a way that is foreign to others. However, it is also important to identify and release anyone that has reinforced these false beliefs.

Questions for Contemplation:
* What or who has made you feel you do not deserve to be loved?

* Can you forgive them?

* What or who has made you feel as if you were fundamentally flawed?

* Can you forgive them?

* What do you need to let go of? What do you need to hold on to?

* What do you truly love?

Cultivating Authentic Wildness

When your divine purpose is truly flowing, you can learn to exist in multiple places at once: chasing ideas in your mind while still remaining aware of your physical surroundings. This is a tricky balance to strike. Having a direct link to multi-dimensional consciousness makes it difficult for most Convergers to stay present. Try creating intentional time during your week for activities that allow you to ponder while simultaneously being present.

I recommend finding something systematic, rhythmic, and creative that you can do with your hands or body while allowing your mind to wander. I know one Converger who paints galaxies and another who writes a daily blog. Other examples include: crocheting, walking to a tempo, practicing EMDR, coloring mandalas, zentangle (structured pattern drawing), hiking, jogging, breath work, beading, jewelry making, tinkering, playing music, and baking. It is important that the task have some physical output. Meditation is not always effective for the Convergers, as they already spend so much time away from their bodies.

Your Fearless Soul

As you cultivate your authentic wildness, face your fears, forgive, and allow your divine purpose to flow, you may notice that:

* You have a tendency to be eccentric and socially odd, but you like it that way!

* You possess a multi-dimensional awareness.

* You are playful and innocent.

* You are inventive and imaginative, and you like to create unique and improbable solutions.

* Others feel an incredible sense of wonder and awe around you.

* Others can walk away from an interaction with you feeling like they have a significant contribution or are uniquely talented.

* You help people recognize what is wonderful and awe-worthy about them.

* You remind people to feel child-like again and give people permission to be weird, odd, and fascinating.

* People find you utterly endearing.

* You are powerfully impactful in ways that are uncommon, intangible, innocent, and sometimes downright odd!

Recommended Exercises for Convergers in Part III

Emotional Flow (p. 127). In the Continued Practice, try using fear or panic in your conversation.

Get Present (p. 131)

Play (p. 133)

PART III

Implementation & Exercises

Tell me what it is you plan to do

with your one wild and precious life?

-Mary Oliver

Chapter 12

THE FEARLESS SOUL SYSTEM

On the morning that I write this, a full moon is rising over the mountains near my home: a fullness of white and mystery hovering over a craggy ridge. It fills me with a profound sense of rightness in the world, a persistent trust that everything flows in accordance with its own divine purpose. The sunflowers stretch their scaly faces to the morning light. The moon circles the earth that circles the sun that circles the center of our Milky Way. The tides move in and out and the leaves fall and return again. It is all free. It is all fearless.

We too can be free and fearless if we trust that our divine purpose will lead us to exactly what we are meant to be. And by being that, we inherently do what we are meant to do. Our struggle lies only in the resisting of our authentic nature. The sunflowers do not deny their draw to the light and the moon does not resist its orbit. We are no different than the sun, the moon, the stars, and the sunflowers. If we surrender to the pull that draws us, we may also experience the profound beauty that is being true to who we are and true to the calling of our Soul.

Of course, a little guidance on *how* to do that on a daily basis is always useful, right?

Daily Practice for Divine Purpose Types

Each divine purpose type has a unique focus question designed to help you return to your wildness. When you are with other people, bored at work, or feel even the slightest bit off center, you can use your focus question to help your divine purpose flow. The focus questions for each type are:

* Initiators: What inspires me right now? Or, what needs to be awoken or ignited?

* Messengers: What is the truth of this moment?

* Believers: What do I believe in this moment?

* Conduits: What is my Soul longing for? And what is being longed for by others?

* Guardians: What do I enjoy right now? Or, what do I value?

* Seers: What do I see?

* Convergers: Is this person connected to me? And what new reality is needed?

You do not have to answer your focus question, although when answers do surface, they are always interesting. It is more important to ask the question silently to yourself and notice what changes occur internally and externally. Many people, including me, notice that simply asking the question cultivates a sense of calm and inner peace. You may find this is true for you, or you may notice other responses such as inspiration, hope, and presence. Your response to the focus question will be as unique as you are.

Your focus questions, and the entire Fearless Soul System for that matter, are not set in stone. Everything in this book is intended to be flexible so that you can define your divine purpose for yourself. Your focus question is meant to be molded and shaped until it reaches the sweet spot where you feel it is "yours." When you sense Soul-to-Soul interaction, the deep connection of spirit between you and another, this is when you know that your focus question has become your own. So play with your focus question. Try it out in different scenarios: at the dog park, in the shower, inside cubicle walls, with children. Be curious and see what happens. Listen to the whispers of your Soul and have the courage to follow them.

The most important thing to remember is that divine purpose is a practice. Knowing your divine purpose doesn't automatically change the course of your life or alter your circumstances. Simply typing yourself and others doesn't create lasting change. Deliberate effort, concerted focus, attention, and practice are what bring lasting change.

Many people I've worked with have told me that it can take anywhere from six months to a year to comprehend the full impact of their divine purpose. I do not tell you this to discourage you from trying, but to encourage you to keep going. Keep practicing your divine purpose and find opportunities to give your gift wherever you can! It will take tremendous courage to claim who you are and your divine purpose in the world. You will have to choose every day to proclaim and fight for who you are. It is only by daring to be more of who we are that can we be free. Only then are we truly Fearless Souls.

What's Next for Your Fearless Soul

"There is in god, some say, a deep but dazzling darkness." -Henry Vaughan

Like the petals of a flower, your divine purpose unfolds from the bud and exposes itself to you. First your primary type emerges, and then your secondary and tertiary purposes follow suit, softly freeing your fullest expression. This continues until all seven types have opened into wholeness, like a rose completely in bloom. When this happens, you are entering the phase of inclusion. When just one divine purpose type doesn't feel right all the time, it is time to expand and include.

Go back and read the divine purpose chapters where you feel resistance. Where was there an absence of resonance or connection? Then try on that type for awhile. Wear it like a winter coat wrapped tight against your skin. Take the time to work through the questions of forgiveness, practices for wildness, and fears for the divine purpose type you have chosen. Utilize its focus question in your daily practice as well. Feel into it. See the world through that type's eyes.

When you have completed all seven divine purpose types in this manner, you can move freely between the focus questions, applying the one most aligned with the moment you find yourself in. This will help you move into what I call the 8th divine purpose type. The 8th divine purpose type uses all seven types at the same time.

That may sound impossible and maybe over stimulating. How do you be seven things at once? The answer is waiting for us, if we only ask the question. The deeper we go into each type, the more it reveals itself. Like deep pools that slowly divulge their secrets as we descend, there is no bottom; each meets the other in the magnificent and dazzling darkness of the deep.

What's down there, I wonder.

Shall we find out together?

Chapter 13

P R A C T I C E S

The following exercises were referenced throughout the divine purpose chapters in Part II. Although some exercises are better suited to certain divine purpose types, anyone can benefit from them. Complete any exercise that compels you. They are presented below in alphabetical order:

1. 1,000 Permissions

2. Boundaries

3. Emotional Flow

4. Energy Accounting

5. Get Present

6. Play

7. Red Ball (An Exercise in Attention)

8. Surrender

9. Spend Time in Nature

1,000 Permissions

By the time most of us reach adulthood, we have conditioned ourselves to silence our desires. We learn in childhood how we *should* behave and what we must *not* do. Many of us have forgotten how to want and desire. In order to return to our authentic wildness, we must begin to listen once more to the gentle impulses of our Souls. In order to get to that level of connection with our Soul's desire, we must walk through the gateway of permission. The journey toward Soul fulfillment begins with a single permission.

Whenever words like "should," "shouldn't," "can't," "won't," or "could've" come into your mind, practice reframing the sentences. Start each sentence with the words "I give myself permission to. . ."

* I give myself permission to. . . have ice cream.

* I give myself permission to. . . ask that stranger on a date.

* I give myself permission to. . . go out and have a good time.

* I give myself permission to. . . go to bed early.

* I give myself permission to. . . take care of my body.

* I give myself permission to. . . spend the day with my children.

You do not have to follow through with every permission. In fact, this could lead to quite a mess! The point of this exercise is to open your mind to the idea that *you are allowed to have what you want.* Give yourself 1,000 permissions until the idea sinks in. How will you know when you have reached 1,000? You won't! The idea is to give yourself permission until you no longer have to.

Continued Practice: Connect with Your Deepest Desires
Using a computer or a pen and paper, complete the following sentence: "I want. . . ."

Find numerous ways to finish this sentence. As you write, try not to judge the things on your list. Simply list each desire moving through your system—even the ones you may consider superficial or silly. For example your list may start like this:

* I want. . . more money.

* I want. . . to be in shape.

* I want. . . more time off work.

Eventually, your answers will begin to transition from surface-level desires to the deep desires of your Soul. You will know when you have reached a Soul desire because a physical sensation or emotional response will ensue: tears, chills, increased heart rate, laughter, etc. When you hit a visceral response, stop. Pay attention to the desire that evoked the response. Your deep desire may sound something like:

* I want. . . to be loved.

* I want. . . to be free.

* I want. . . to help.

The desires of your Soul will be all your own. The list above is meant to be an example and a starting place.

Boundaries

A boundary is just a guideline, a helpful demarcation that supports satisfying your needs. Clarity around your needs will identify boundaries. Here are some important questions to consider:

* What do you need to feel safe?
* What do you need to feel connected to someone?
* What do you need to feel connected with yourself?
* How much time do you need to re-fill your tanks?
* What do you need from your friendships?
* What do you need in order to trust someone?
* What do you need to fall asleep at night?
* What do you need in order to feel productive and useful during the day?

Answering these questions honestly is wonderful, but unless you make practical and tangible changes to your life, the exercise will have been meaningless. So what boundaries should you put in place in order to satisfy the needs uncovered in the previous questions? For example, do you need the boundary of a 9 o'clock bedtime to satisfy your sleeping need, or the boundary of clear goals to satisfy the need of feeling useful?

It is important to note that while boundaries do move and change, they are like a shifting mountain range. The shift happens slowly and with deliberate consideration. Boundaries are not rules set in stone. They are merely markers to help you identify what is a good idea for you and what will contribute your ultimate happiness *at this point in time*. Five years from now, those needs may change because you will have changed. It is a good idea to return to this exercise every now and again to determine if there are new needs and, subsequently, new boundaries.

Emotional Flow

Emotions are meant to be felt. Bottled-up emotions are harmful to our internal systems and distance us from the present moment. Learn to let your emotions flow, whatever they may be.

Remember that emotions are never "bad." They are merely messages conveying information about the current state of your Soul. The more skillful you become in handling your emotions, the more effectively you can navigate your divine purpose.

The trick to working through your emotional states—especially if you are experiencing some of the darker emotions, such as grief or despair—is to acknowledge what you feel. Name and welcome the emotion instead of denying it. Feel it all the way; let yourself respond.

Remember that you do not need to *act* on every dark thought or emotion. You must simply acknowledge it. Turn your focus to your body, noticing the emotions and sensations that are present. Allow the thoughts and emotions[6] to pass through you, watching them go by like a train on its tracks, and let them go.

Continued Practice: Conversation with Emotions

If you are struggling with what it means to let your emotions flow, try this exercise. Grab a pen and paper. Pretend that the emotion in question is a person and give it a name. I like the idea of naming my more difficult emotions "Dark Christin" because they appear in my imagination as darker versions of myself. Begin by drawing a line down the middle of the page. On the left, write your name. Label the right column with the name of your emotion. Then, to begin the conversation, pose a question to your darker self. Allow the answers on the right side of the column to come naturally. Try not to think too hard. Let the emotion guide you. As you write, remember to have compassion for your darker self: it is trying to tell you something important.

For example the conversation could look like this:

---

[6] Emotional advice given in this book is based on Karla McLaren's book *The Language of Emotions: What Your Feelings Are Trying to Tell You*. For in-depth information about how to work with each emotion, I highly recommend her writings, workshops, and books (www.karlamclaren.com).

Christin	Dark Christin
Why are you angry?	I'm pissed because all this hard stuff is happening, and I can't fix it or control it.
That sounds terrible. What do you want to do about it?	I want to punch someone in the face!
Totally get that! Would that make you feel better?	Not really. I think I just need some time to myself to think through all these big things. It's too much to handle and I'm overwhelmed. I need to feel connected to myself in order to make any worthwhile decisions.
Wow. That makes so much sense. How should we do that?	Can we call in sick tomorrow?
I don't think so. You know how my boss gets weird about that. What if I blocked off the next few evenings and the entire weekend? No social engagements or appointments, just quiet recovery and reflection time. Would that be okay?	Yes.

In this example Dark Christin is feeling angry and overwhelmed, and it is very wise for her to recoup. I hope I listen to her!

Energy Accounting

Energy accounting is just what it sounds like: taking account of your energy levels. Depending on your circumstances, your energy levels are constantly increasing or decreasing. After every interaction with a person, group, or task, ask yourself, "Do I feel better or worse?" It is important to ask yourself this question *after* the interaction or activity. Sometimes we convince ourselves that we aren't going to enjoy something, like working out or visiting Grandma, when the truth is that it will make us feel better. Likewise, activities we believe we should enjoy may result in a negative accounting when reflected upon afterwards. Keep track of whether your energy increases or decreases after activities and interactions. Your time is best spent with people who make you feel better and with tasks that energize you. Let go of the people and situations that make you feel worse.

There will be some unpleasant areas that you cannot eliminate—spending time with your boss, for example, or paying bills. The question then becomes, "What can I do to make this a more enjoyable experience?"

For example: I hate paying bills. To improve the experience, I try to have a delicious spritzer and a piece of dark chocolate during bill-paying time. After I pay each bill online or write a check, I sip my spritzer and nibble my chocolate. Then I take a moment to thank the service I am paying for, out loud. When I pay rent, I say, "Thank you for this beautiful home. I love where I live." For the Internet bill, I say, "Thank you for keeping me connected to my clients, family, and friends." I still don't love paying bills, but the experience is now more enjoyable than just straight up hate.

This method is trickier when it comes to people because you cannot control their behavior. When dealing with an unpleasant person, try focusing your attention on something calm. Use the Red Ball exercise (page 135) to help train your attention. Place the red ball on something pleasant in your vicinity, like a tree, a nice color, or the nicest person in the room. It takes practice to do this without looking like you are more interested in a house plant than the intolerable person, but you will get better at it and it will make the experience more enjoyable. Just keep practicing.

You may not always be able to bring your energy levels back into the positive, but try to adjust the circumstance so that your energy accounting has a return of neutral. Remember, you have the power to change your experience.

Continued Practice: Big Rocks First

If you wanted to fill a jar with assorted rocks, you'd put the big rocks in first to make sure they fit. Smaller pebbles would fill in the cracks. Do the same with your energy accounting. Think of three to five activities that fill your energy tanks—tasks that make you feel like yourself. These could be anything from fixing your car to drinking beers with the guys, sitting on the porch to being out in nature. These are your big rocks, so they should be the most important things on your to-do list.

The smaller rocks are your daily to-do's: everything you must do to keep your life moving forward. These include activities like grocery shopping, laundry, and picking up the kids from school. You will have plenty of energy to complete these tasks if you take the time to fill your tanks beforehand. The problem occurs when we make the pebbles our priority.

Big rocks come first.

Get Present

Presence refers to full-body awareness. This involves receptivity through the senses and intimate communion with your internal and external circumstances. To practice presence, complete each of the following sentences three times out loud:

* I see. . .

* I hear. . .

* I smell. . .

* I taste. . .

* I feel on my skin. . .

* I know. . .

You want your sentences to be simplified versions of what you perceive. Stick with the basics and be specific. For example, say "I see one white rectangle" as opposed to "I see my computer." Similarly, "I hear high-pitched buzzing" is more specific than "I hear the refrigerator." Break your responses down into shapes, colors, and sensations. This may be difficult, especially when it comes to tastes and smells, but with practice your senses will expand and improve.

For example:

* I see. . . two black rectangles, one blue circle, and one flat, grey surface.

* I hear. . . flute sounds. I hear ripping. I hear voices.

* I smell. . . something burnt. I smell coffee. I smell skin.

* I taste. . . the back of my teeth. I taste numbness on the middle of my tongue. I taste coolness in the back of my throat.

* I feel on my skin. . . smoothness under my fingers. I feel lightweight fabric across my shoulders. I feel pressure in my left heel.

* I know. . . that I am going to be O.K. I know that I am loved. I know that I am safe.

Now you try.

When you are finished, ask yourself: How do I feel compared to when I started? What do I notice? Try this exercise anytime you don't feel present, grounded, or connected to your authentic wildness.

Continued Practice: Presence requires that you focus on your current experience. A helpful trick is to speak and think only in present tense: "I am breathing"; "I am sitting in a chair"; "I hear the sound of traffic"; "I feel strange"; etc. Pay attention to what is happening right now. This will help steer your body and mind into the present moment.

Play

To play is to do something that has no point or end goal. Sometime this week, find time to play. Do something without a point for at least twenty minutes. A lot of people don't know how to play, so here is a list of activities that have no point or goal to get your juices flowing. Laugh, enjoy, and feel your Soul get lighter and lighter!

* Play a card game, board game, or mind game.

* Go for a walk and get lost.

* Watch clouds and make up the shapes.

* Hum, sing, or whistle.

* Play a musical instrument (even if you don't know how).

* Draw or paint.

* Color.

* Ride a bike.

* Ride a scooter.

* Build a fort.

* Build something using scrap wood or other materials lying about.

* Make origami.

* Bake.

* Knit.

* Play around with your tools.

* Look through car magazines.

* Have a pull-up or pushup competition.

* Cook something without a recipe.

* Write a story.

* Tell a story with two or more people (each person only gets to say one word at a time).

* Do cartwheels or somersaults.

* Play "Red Light Green Light."

* Dance. (Yes, even if you look like a fool.)

* Play tag.

* See how many steps it takes you to cross a field, taking large steps.

* See how many steps it takes you to cross a field, taking baby steps.

* Make something up!

Red Ball (An Exercise in Attention)

Attention is powerful, but it is difficult to explain because it isn't tangible. Even though attention isn't something we can touch, it is something we can feel. We intuitively know whether someone is paying attention to us or not. We can even sense when someone is watching us from across the room. Attention refers to the place or time where your concentration is being directed.

This exercise uses an imaginary red bouncy ball as the focus of your attention. The red ball gives you something tangible to focus on, helping draw your attention to a specific point, which can help you listen to your heart and Soul. Wherever your attention lies, is the place from which you connect to others. If your attention is on the heart, you will connect to others from the heart. If your attention is on your mind—or elsewhere entirely—you will connect to others from that place.

Like any skill, attention can be honed. We must train ourselves to focus our attention so that we can more regularly hear the whispers of Soul.

Take this little red ball in your mind right now and imagine it in different locations in the room you now occupy. Place it in the corner, in the middle of the ceiling, or on the left side of the floor. Roll it over your toes and up the back of your spine. Let the ball come to rest in the middle of your forehead.

* Keeping your attention on the red ball in the middle of your forehead, complete the sentence "I want _____."

* Move the red ball down to your heart cavity. If it helps, place your hand over your heart to feel your heart beat. Keeping your attention on the red ball in the middle of your heart, complete the sentence again: "I want _____."

* Now roll the red ball down to just below your belly button. Keeping your attention on the red ball in your lower abdomen, complete the sentence one last time: "I want _____."

Try not to judge or explain the answers to yourself. Just allow the responses to arise naturally from each location. The first thing that pops up into your awareness is usually correct. It could be anything from "I want a grilled cheese sandwich" to "I want world peace." The best way to start training your attention is to notice the subtle differences that occur depending on where your attention is placed.

A nice little trick to focus attention on Soul is to place the red ball where you feel the calmest in your body. As an alternate, you could place it on the part of your body that feels the most sensation. What do you notice about your answers when your attention is focused in different areas of your body?

Continued Practice

Use the Red Ball in conversations where you want to create more intimacy. Image the red ball in your throat, heart, stomach, or even the bottom of your feet—anywhere lower than your brain—and speak with your attention on that spot. Don't think. Don't formulate. Just place your attention somewhere on your body, open your mouth, and say something. Many people find this practice to be extremely vulnerable. It is meant to be. This is why I call it "advanced." Share only when you are ready, but do share!

Surrender

Surrender is not giving up. Rather, surrender implies that you put your faith in something greater than yourself. That "something greater" doesn't need to be God or a particular ideal; it can be as simple as surrendering to a dream, to love, to the process, or to your own heart and its gentle whispers. Spend time communing with the magical, the mystical, and the mysterious. Look for that "something greater" in the world around you. Notice what moves your spirit, calls to your heart, and resonates with your Soul.

That "something greater" is everywhere. Turn your attention to it, get curious about the way it moves and breaths, and let it guide you. This is a very personal practice, and I do not intend to make assumptions about what will be spiritual for you. Think about what makes you feel humble, sacred, and a part of a greater story on the planet, and do *whatever that is as regularly as possible.*

The key to surrender is letting go. For now, try clenching your fists as tightly as you can and simultaneously inhaling to the fullest extent of your lungs. When you lungs are full, keep clenching your fists and count to three. Then exhale slowly and release your hands. When your lungs are empty, keep your hands soft and count to three. Repeat the cycle three times. Each time you exhale and relax, think of one thing you want to let go of. It could be anger, fear, doubt, delusion, lust, lost love, money, attachment, etc. Imagine it departing with the tension in your hands. When we let go of things that do not serve us, we make room in our lives for the things that will. We create space for that "something greater" to move through us.

Continued Practice: Equanimity and Ultimate Surrender

Think back to some of the terrible and unfortunate things that have happened to you in the past few years. Maybe you got kicked out of your house, or a close friend died suddenly. Perhaps you didn't get the job you wanted, or someone took credit for your work. When all was said and done, when the dust had settled, were you ever in a *worse* position than before? Probably not. You may have felt worse—death, loss, and theft are not easy to deal with, after all!—but you learned and grew. *You were changed somehow by the chaos.*

The "something greater" does not label any circumstance "good" or "bad"—humans do that. When something hurts, we call it bad, but it is really just chaos. When something feels good, we call it perfection, but it is really just the order that occurs after chaos. Surrendering is about letting go when there is chaos and when there is perfection. You are not the designer or the creator of the universe, but you have a choice. You can choose to trust that after every storm there is a rainbow. After every heartache and upheaval, we always come back to perfection and order—often with more simplicity, relief, and deeper understanding of ourselves.

Spend Time in Nature

Nature does not lie: the storms, sun, wind, and snow are not subversions of the truth; they just *are*. Imagine that the earth, sun, clouds, and wind have personalities, and imagine what they might say to you. Ask questions of nature and imagine the answers. For example, if this tree could talk, I imagine it would tell me not to worry about my boss. It would tell me to stay true to myself. Imagine that nature has a voice and something powerful and real to say to you. As you imagine this infinite knowing, take note of your sensations, feelings, and intuitions. How does it feel in your body when nature speaks to you?

It is also helpful for each divine purpose type to spend time in nature seeking the following:

* Initiators: new life

* Messengers: truth

* Believers: what is growing or mending

* Conduits: what is reproducing or attracting

* Guardians: what is being protected or valued

* Seers: patterns in chaos

* Convergers: new realities

APPENDIX A

WHAT IS A SOUL?

It is important to me that I use terms and vocabulary accurately. One term in particular requires careful exploration, as it forms the very foundation of this book. Partway through the writing process, therefore, I set out to answer the question: What is a Soul?

There are varied beliefs about what a Soul is and whether it exists at all. The traditional Inuit cultures of Northern America conceived of a multi-part soul: one part died with the body, one part proceeded to an afterlife, and the third remained on earth to guide the descendants of the tribe. The Egyptians and the Chinese conceived of a dual soul: one part died with the body and another part proceeded to an afterlife of some kind. The Early Hebrews did not separate soul from body. Later Christian theology split the material and immaterial, making the body and soul separate. In Hinduism, the soul is the eternal self. Buddhism negates the concept of individual self and soul all together ("Soul").

Most belief structures hold that some part of our identity is impermanent. Still, throughout my research, it became apparent that no one *knows* for sure whether there is such a thing as a Soul. This was upsetting to me and spun me into what can only be described as a mini-spiritual crisis. How could I write about a thing that didn't have tangible evidence—something that couldn't be quantified or agreed upon?

I finally concluded that what mattered, at least in the context of this book, was what Soul meant to *me*. I turned to the natural world for an appropriate metaphor to describe my concept of Soul, and the images of black holes kept bubbling into my consciousness.

A black hole is a collapsed star whose gravitational field has become so dense and compact that even light cannot escape. No one has ever actually *seen* a black hole: they are undetectable to the naked eye. Even x-rays or other forms of electromagnetic radiation cannot find them or look into them ("Black Holes"). The only way to locate a black hole is "to look for matter that is orbiting what seems to be an unseen compact massive object" (Hawking 115–116). In other words, black holes can only be observed based on the effects they produce on their nearby environment.

The Soul, I believe, is much like the black hole. That may sound dark and depressing, but black holes are actually magnificent and mysterious. They are, scientists believe, the very reason galaxies can exist (Hawking 116). They are life-giving and beautiful, but we cannot observe them directly with modern technology. Just as we know black holes exist because of their effects, I have come to believe that the Soul exists based on my experience of its effects: in this case, divine purpose.

It is not my intention to undermine any beliefs about what a Soul is or to challenge anyone's religious or spiritual vantage point. My intention is to define the Soul as I understand it in order to provide deeper insight into the nature of a divine purpose. *For the purpose of this book, I refer to the Soul as a system.*

The body, mind, emotions, intuition, and that mysterious, tenacious, and creative force called "life" all work together to form what I call the Soul.

Whatever the impermanent part of us is, it does not fully exist without a body to be in, emotions to express it, a mind to understand it, and a vision to have faith in its connection to something *greater*. The Soul is a balanced system, an interconnected network of components that all equally rely upon and contribute to the whole of our human experience.

When a person is missing one of these components, it isn't that they don't have a Soul. If someone is in a coma or has decreased emotional capacity, do they have a Soul? If they are missing a piece of their body, do they have a Soul? If someone does not believe in some greater power, do they have a Soul? Most people would intuitively say, "Of course!"

However if we remove and isolate that brain or that emotion, does it have a Soul? What if you remove a pair of eyes, a nose, a single hair, or one atomic molecule: does it have a Soul? No one knows for sure, but probably not. It is the *joining* of our intellect, emotions, physical sensations, and spirituality that creates the system, and it is the system that creates the imprint called a divine purpose.

In the end, it was a meaningful exercise to decide what the concept of Soul meant to me and it helped inform the whole of this work. As you consider my definition, dear reader, I trust you to follow your instincts. If you feel called, consider for yourself what you believe the Soul to be.

APPENDIX B

R E S O U R C E S

Some of these resources were credited directly in the text and others were not. All of them contributed to my own personal healing, and I have found them to be invaluable voices guiding me along my path.

Books and Publications

Haines, Staci. *The Survivor's Guide to Sex: How to Have an Empowered Sex Life after Child Sexual Abuse*. San Francisco: Cleis Press, 1999. Print.

Lief, Judith L. *Making Friends with Death: A Buddhist Guide to Encountering Mortality*. Boston: Shambhala Publications, 2001. Print.

McLaren, Karla. *The Language of Emotions: What Your Feelings Are Trying to Tell You*. Boulder: Sounds True, 2010. Print.

---. *The Art of Empathy: A Complete Guide to Life's Most Essential Skill*. Boulder: Sounds True, 2013. Print.

Plotkin, Bill. *Nature and the Human Soul: Cultivating Wholeness and Community in a Fragmented World*. Novato, CA: New World Library, 2008. Print.

Schwartz, Richard C. *Internal Family Systems Therapy*. New York: The Guilford Press, 1995. Print.

Spilsbury, Ariel. *The 13 Moon Oracle: Holographic Meditations on the Mystery*. San Francisco: Mandala Publishing, 2006. Print.

Thompson, Mary Reynolds. *Reclaiming the Wild Soul: How Earth's Landscapes Restore Us to Wholeness*: White Cloud Press, 2014. Print.

Woititz, Janet Geringer. *Adult Children of Alcoholics*. Deerfield Beach, FL: Health Communications, 1983. Print.

Other Resources
Adverse Childhood Experiences Exam
Ten questions designed to take a rough measure of difficult childhood experiences linking them to long-term health and social consequences.
http://www.acestudy.org/

Coaches Training Institute
Leadership training and development.
http://www.thecoaches.com/

Happy
Documentary film about the components of happiness and contentment.
www.thehappymovie.com

Headspace
An easy and useful meditation app for smart phones.
https://www.headspace.com/

APPENDIX C

FREQUENTLY ASKED QUESTIONS

There are a handful of questions that come up consistently after people learn about the seven divine purpose types. The questions and their answers are listed below.

Am I born with my divine purpose?

We come into the world with inherent traits, and our divine purpose is woven into the fabric of who we are. Our authentic wildness develops and grows from this foundation, but at some point in every person's life, authentic wildness and divine purpose get shut down. It is during this time that we can learn to utilize some of the other divine purpose types for survival. Add social conditioning, our understanding of our world, and the events of our past into the mix, and we get who we are today.

So, yes, we are born with our divine purpose type. This does not mean, however, that we cannot adopt new traits as we learn and grow.

Can I have more than one divine purpose type?

The short answer is that we have access to all seven types at all times.

That being said, there will be one divine purpose type that flows most effortlessly and joyously, one type that is your orientation and source of aliveness at all times. We all have secondary (and even tertiary) types, but they will be in service of your primary divine purpose type.

Example A: I am a Seer with Converger as my secondary type. When I look into something or someone, a pattern emerges (Seer). This pattern usually floats around like a bunch of puzzle pieces until, *wham!*—they snap together to form some kind of alternate perspective or shift (Converger). These "puzzle pieces" do their thing in service of the Seer divine purpose and ultimately create harmony and balance.

Example B: One of my dear friends is an Initiator with strong Conduit and Messenger types as her secondary and tertiary. She is oriented toward awakening people's potential at all times. However, she is also able to help people identify what will truly fulfill them (Conduit), to attract the resources to do so (also Conduit), and to help them tell the truth to themselves (Messenger). The uncovering of desire and truth are in service to the Initiator type, and ultimately they help people cross thresholds and become a greater version of themselves.

Example C: Another loved one is a Believer with strong Guardian as her secondary. She is oriented toward growth, wholeness, and leadership at all times. However, she is also able to identify what is precious and valuable in others (Guardian) and help them feel longed for by the whole (also Guardian). Identifying what is valuable and precious helps her build something for the greater good.

We are all able to access all seven divine purpose types. They each flow within us, but there will be one that compels us most.

Can my divine purpose change?

I believe our divine purposes can change, but not in the way we might think. They don't change like a linear jump from one lily pad to the next, nor do they change like a pair of old clothes. We don't grow out of one and into another.

Our divine purpose includes as it expands; it matures and develops to embrace the other types. We blossom into the wholeness of all the gifts as we progress in our ability to wield our own divine purpose.

Are there more than seven types?

Probably. The Fearless Soul System is seen through my particular lens from my particular circumstances, but I am completely willing to accept that there are more than these seven. The seven types are based merely on my experiences with others. How exciting to discover more!

A couple of other notes:

It is difficult to know your true divine purpose during a major transition, such as the death of a loved one, divorce, or a new job. I have noticed that when people's lives are in upheaval, they have a tendency to mis-type themselves. This isn't necessarily wrong; it may just mean we rely on other types as a form of survival mask. If you are in transition, I recommend coming back to this work when the transition is complete and see for yourself if your divine purpose type has changed or not.

A second group that has difficulty with this system is people living in a land that is different than their country of origin. If this is the case for you:

it helps to recall memories of childhood in your homeland. Using those memories seems to help for discovering both your authentic wildness traits and divine purpose classification.

Another group that this system doesn't entirely work for those rare humans who have entered eldership. If adolescence is about tending to your own Soul, and adulthood is about tending to the Soul of other, then eldership is about tending to the Soul of the world. There are very few elders in the world anymore: they are precious and rare, and just because someone is aged doesn't mean that they have reached true eldership. However, when trying to type someone in eldership, I have noticed that they have difficulty picking just one. I believe this goes back to the "expand and include" scenario listed previously. I believe that the types grow into and overlap each other until they become one cohesive purpose and act as an indicator of eldership.

WORKS CITED

Works Cited in Part I

"Forgive." *Etymonline.com*. Online etymology dictionary, 2001. <www. etymonline. com/index.php>

Harlow, Harry F., and Stephen J. Suomi. "Induced Psychopathology in Monkeys." *Engineering and Science* 33.6 (1970). Full article: <http://calteches.library.caltech.edu/2803/1/monkeys.pdf]]>

Schwartz, Richard C. *Introduction to the Internal Family Systems Model*. Oak Park, IL: Trailheads, 2001. Print.

Thomas, Alexander, Stella Chess, and Herbert G. Birch. "The Origin of Personality." *Scientific American* (1970).

Works Cited in Part II

"American civil rights movement". *Encyclopædia Britannica*. Encyclopædia Britannica Online.

"Belief." *Etymonline.com*. Online etymology dictionary, 2001. <www. etymonline. com/index.php>

"Biography of Nelson Mandela." *Nelson Mandela Foundation*. Web. 19 Sept. 2015. <https://www.nelsonmandela.org/content/page/biography>.

Chesterton, G. K., and Alzina Stone Dale. *Chesterton on Dickens*. San Francisco: Ignatius, 1989. Print. (246)

"Come to the Edge", from *New Numbers* (London: Jonathan Cape, 1969) pp. 65-66.

"Compassion." *Etymonline.com*. Online etymology dictionary, 2001. <www. etymonline. com/index.php>

"Dorothea Lange." The Biography Channel website, 2014. 6 Mar. 2014, 11:18 http://www.biography.com/people/dorothea-lange-9372993.

"Initiation." *Etymonline.com*. Online etymology dictionary, 2001. <www. etymonline. com/index.php>

Lee, Richard B., and Richard Daly. "Introduction: Foragers and Others." Introduction. *The Cambridge Encyclopedia of Hunters and Gatherers*. Cambridge: Cambridge UP, 1999. Print.

Nature 391 (1998): 871-874. Web. 25 Sept. 2015.

O'Shaughnessy, Arthur (4 October 1873). "An Ode". Appleton's Journal (New York, NY: D. Appleton & Company).

Whyte, David. "Sweet Darkness." *The House of Belonging* Many Rivers Press, 1997. Print.

Works Cited in Part III
"Black Holes." *NASA Science*. NASA. Web. 05 Nov. 2014. Full article: <http://science.nasa.gov/astrophysics/focus-areas/black-holes/>

Hawking, Stephen. *The Universe in a Nutshell*. New York: Bantam, 2001. Print.

McLaren, Karla. *The Art of Empathy*. Sounds True, 2013.

Oliver, Mary. "The Summer Day." *New and Selected Poems, Volume One*. Boston, MA: Beacon, 1992. N. pag. Print.

"Soul". *Encyclopædia Britannica. Encyclopædia Britannica Online.* Encyclopædia Britannica Inc., 2015. Web. 26 Sept. 2015. http://www.britannica.com/topic/soul-religion-and-philosophy

Botanical illustrations taken from pages (11, 21, 62, 71, 80, 93, 122, and 150) in *The Elements of Botany for Beginners and for Schools* by Asa Gray, New York: American Book Company, 1887. Print.

GRATITUDES

I often end workshops with a circle of "gratitudes." It is a nice way to end the relationship and the time together.

First, I'd like to thank you, dear reader. Thank you for picking up this book, for coming along this journey with me, and for daring to discover your own Fearless Soul. Your wildness and authenticity are what will make this world a better place. Keep going deeper.

To my sweet husband: thank you for loving me through this writing with your never-failing generosity. Thank you for listening to draft, after draft, after draft and encouraging every word. You are my truest love.

To Sheri Smith, who initiated this book into my consciousness: thank you for loving me and my work, and thank you for listening to my (many) meltdowns related (and not related) to this book. Thank you for being gentle when I exclaimed, "I don't know if there is a Soul!" You breathe such sweet life into my spirit.

Marie Campbell: thank you for believing in this book and helping it grow. It is such a beauty because of your editing prowess and tender heart. You have made this whole experience wonderful, and I will look back on our time together with fondness.

Diane Israel: without your mentorship I would never have aligned with my wildness and authenticity at all.

Auntie K. Kimsey-House: thank you for calls that kept me on track and encouragement when I got off track. Thank you for my very first lesson in helping flowers to grow.

Uncle H. Kimsey-House: thank you for reminding me to turn inward, looking to my body sensations for answers.

To the readers of the first draft, Colten, Ben, and Cybelle: your gentle and loving feedback gave me the courage to keep going. Thank you.

Scott Smith: thank you for your faith in me and for letting your wife and me throw numerous experimental Fearless Soul workshops (which look more like dinner parties) in your home. We had such fun!

To my second draft readers, Juliet, Alyse, Layla, David, and John Lee: your refinements made the content truly remarkable. It has a shine to it that it just didn't before. Mhuah!

Kriste Peoples: thank you for your badass clarity and contagious laughter. Also, thank you for ultimately coining the term "divine purpose." Remind me to tell you about it sometime.

Many thanks to Sabina Spencer, whose exquisite insight crystallized the layout of this book.

Rachel Thor: thank you for your amazing ability to attract diverse people to intimate gatherings. They changed the content multiple times over. Just like your name, you are a thunder goddess.

Momma and Dan: thank you for rushing to my devastated side when someone else trademarked my original typing system name. Your support and belief in me helped me push through and find a new (and infinitely better) title. Yay!

Dad and Julee: thank you for a lifetime of love and support. You are my squishy-nougat center.

To my sibling clan: thank you for making me smile along the way.

Summer Smith: thank you for your words that reminded me numerous times while writing to come home to myself.

Red Viper Squad: I couldn't have written the last chapters without our game. Thank you so much for playing.

Skye Kerr: thank you for your compassionate and lovely final editing touches and for ushering me through completion resistance.

To the many, many people who participated in workshops, conversations, emails, lunches, office hallway discussions, and after-work happy hours that contributed to the content: thank you. There are too many names to list, but you made this book the beauty that it is.

I am grateful.

Are you interested in:

Throwing on your own Fearless Soul workshop or party?
Sharing with your book club?
Learning to type divine purpose in others?
Using the content in your work?

Fearless Soul System Resources and Materials are available at:

www.ChristinMyrick.com